THE
MIS ING
PEACE

The Mis

Peace b

Jared N

sing
y
eman

Hardcover: 979-8-9854913-0-2
Paperback: 979-8-9854913-1-9
Audiobook: 979-8-9854913-2-6
Ebook: 979-8-9854913-3-3

First edition January 2022

Book Design by Aidan James Agency
Printed by El Paso Mail and Print Service

CSJ Ministries, Inc.
1000 Valley Crest Dr
El Paso, TX 79907

JaredNieman.com

Manufactured in the United States of America

Table of Contents

MARCOS WITT
Foreword
I–III

CHAPTER 1
Are You Okay?
1–11

CHAPTER 2
The Missing Peace
13–22

CHAPTER 3
Battle for Your Soul
25–35

CHAPTER 4
Guarding Your Heart
37–48

CHAPTER 5
Don't Lose Heart
51–60

CHAPTER 6
A Fresh Start
63–71

CHAPTER 7
Take A Stand
73–85

CHAPTER 8
Shame No More   87–94

CHAPTER 9
In the Face of   97–107
Disappointment

CHAPTER 10
Turning   109–120
Disappointment
Into Victory

CHAPTER 11
The Power of Vision   123–131

CHAPTER 12
You Are A   133–143
Masterpiece!

CHAPTER 13
Not A Copy   145–154

CHAPTER 14
On Purpose,   157–170
For A Purpose

CHAPTER 15
Cherished, Valued,   173–182
Loved

CHAPTER 16
What Are You   185–197
Thinking?

CHAPTER 17
Winning the Battle   199–209
in Your Mind

CHAPTER 18
Positive or   211–223
Negative?

CHAPTER 19
Joy and Happiness   225–235

CHAPTER 20
Trust the Process   237–245

Foreword

MARCOS WITT

We all need peace— no matter how much of it we think we have, we need or desire, don't we? Why wouldn't anyone want more peace? There is nothing better than living life with lots of it. The confidence, security and boldness that peace affords is what gives us the strength to face each day with a calm determination, no matter what might come our way. It is a powerful and helpful companion in our walk through life.

In a world where stress seems to govern so many, it is imperative that we understand how to allow peace to rule our thoughts, conversations, decisions, and relationships; there are countless studies that prove how stress is ruining our lives. Entire warehouses could be filled with the data produced by them, and yet, the bottom line of each study is the same: Our world needs peace! How did the most comfortable and prosperous age in the history of mankind become so anxious and stressful? It is literally eating away at society like an aggressive cancer, destroying everything in its path. Countless marriages, families, friendships, neighbors, relationships have been destroyed because of stress. There is a massive void in the soul of humankind that can best be described as "The Missing Peace."

When I met Jared Nieman several years ago, he was quite "put together." He was already married to his beautiful wife, Karla, a father to their two children, and actively involved at his father's side as one of the main leaders and pastors of the incredible church they serve. As the years have gone by, I am continually impressed by his growth and development, both in leadership skills as well as in the outstanding public communication gift he possesses. I openly admit that I have, on more than one occasion, lifted illustrations and sermon points from his messages to use as my own. I'm not embarrassed to admit it! A good idea, illustration and/or research is worthy of being repeated. I have had the experience of listening to Jared speak... Time and time again, I'm moved as his voice is being used by God to encourage, strengthen and comfort me; Jared is both anointed and empowering as one of the greatest pastors of his generation.

Leaders don't arrive at "put together" without struggles, battles, failures, and mistakes from which they learn vitally important lessons that, ultimately, make them into who they are. Great leaders are keenly aware of the power these lessons will have in helping others learn from the mistakes they've made, so they share them openly. In the process, they make themselves vulnerable to their audience while drinking from a cup of humility that small-minded leaders try hard to avoid. I am thankful that in this book, Jared decides to open up his heart by sharing some of his challenges. It takes a confident, self-assured person to speak about their failures. Instead of being talked down to, we are encouraged to become better by learning a lesson from someone who has already learned it the hard way. Reading about some of Jared's shortcomings had two effects on me: 1) Surprise. I never knew he struggled with some of the things he confessed. It was ever so refreshing to know he's just like all the rest of us! 2) Admiration. I respect someone who is brave enough to open themselves up to the possibility of ridicule or criticism in order to help others learn from their mistakes. Bravo, Jared! I've never admired you more than I do now after reading *"The Missing Peace."*

We often hear this word of advice: "Just follow peace." These are such easy words to say but rather difficult to figure out; it is a skill that doesn't come quickly nor easily. In fact, it usually comes well after much trial and error. In this book, Jared lays out helpful, practical insights on following a pathway to peace. One is never "talked down" to but rather, encouraged and strengthened. I felt accompanied as I read. Two friends, on the highway of life, desperately desiring to find peace in the middle of one another's unique and individual storms. Jared walks with us throughout these pages, never with disdain or high-mindedness. Always as a fellow seeker, challenging us and moving us forward in the knowledge that "The Missing Peace" can be found.

There are many great takeaways in this book. No purpose would be served if I made a list of them here. However, I wholeheartedly encourage you to write them down, take actionable steps and reorganize your thoughts around the Biblical principles taught herein. You might want to read a chapter two or three times before moving on, as each one is chock-full of "goodies" for the spirit and soul. I found myself reading certain paragraphs repeatedly as a truth or principle would stand up and make its presence known. I love a book that makes me think deeply and encourages me to pursue the best version of my life possible. This is such a book.

My prayer is that the Prince of Peace will embrace you, your family and your world. When each of us find "The Missing Peace," which can only occur through a personal relationship with Jesus Christ, my hope is that we share it with those around us, allowing God's peace to flow from us to others. That is when our world will have the opportunity to experience His Peace through us. In Matthew 5:16 Jesus says, "let your light shine in such a way that the world may see your good works and glorify the Father" (paraphrased). A very important component to the bright, shining Light of Christ is peace. When the world can see His peace abounding in us, they will glorify the Father which is in Heaven.

Jared's writing comes at the perfect time; I know it will help you. It has already served as a source of encouragement and a blessing to me on a personal level. I am overjoyed to whole-heartedly recommend this book as I'm positive it will touch you. Thank you, Jared, for being vulnerable with us, opening up about your struggles and deep-diving into how the Lord uses your experiences to help you find "The Missing Peace" on a daily basis.

MARCOS WITT

CHAPTER

1

Are You Okay?

THE MISSING PEACE

Are You Okay?

Let me ask you a simple question: **are you okay?** The generic answer we tend to give people would sound something like, "I'm fine" or "Yeah, doing good." Just about every day of our lives, someone will ask how we are doing; but, I wonder how often we answer the question with honesty, rather than just brushing aside the question as a common American greeting to open a meeting or social interaction. If we are all being honest, at some point — maybe even quite often — we lie when we answer the question. Quite often, we are not okay and yet we pretend as if we are. So many people go through their daily lives carrying, and often hiding, a veil of darkness in their hearts and minds. They live with anxiety, shame, depression, panic and suicidal thoughts or tendencies, but are too scared or embarrassed to talk about it. For too long, we have been taught to be ashamed about the fact that we are struggling on the inside. Many people were raised to just push through it, to suck it up, or to simply get over it. This book will empower you with the truth to enable you to win the battle within your soul so you can live healthy mentally, emotionally and spiritually. In every season, we can take control of our hearts, minds and souls to overcome the darkness.

Let me say this before we go any further: I believe being healed or getting better simply starts with being honest. Being honest with yourself, with God, and the people closest to you. We need to remove the stigma of depression, anxiety and mental illness, drop the veil of lies, and enter a place of compassion and understanding for ourselves and people around us who are truly struggling. So, let me ask you again: are you okay?

If you don't know much about me, I am the lead pastor of Abundant Church in El Paso, Texas. My parents, Charles and Rochelle Nieman, founded our amazing church in 1977 and have seen thousands upon thousands of people come into a relationship with Jesus, their lives transformed by developing a personal relationship with God. I have the privilege of serving alongside my sister, Shannon Nieman, as we lead our church into the future with Christ at the forefront of our ministry. I am happily married to a remarkable woman named Karla. She is beautiful, smart, compassionate, generous and loves God with all her heart. Karla is an incredibly successful attorney who manages a demanding career while also being a wonderful mother to our two children, Caleb and Charlotte. To say that I am a blessed man is an understatement, and yet I too have had my struggles with many of the issues we will discuss in the next chapters. Your life being great in appearance does not exempt you from struggling to maintain peace and joy within yourself. Depression and anxiety are indiscriminate as to whom they will attack.

It breaks my heart to see people hurting, longing year-in and year-out to live a life of joy, peace and happiness. As Christians, we are not called by God to live in darkness. Quite the contrary. 1 Peter 2:9 says that God has brought us out of the darkness and into His marvelous light! This is truly one of the greatest blessings God has bestowed upon all of us as His children. The Bible also teaches us that we are blessed to be a blessing. That simply means that God not only wants to bless us to make our lives better, but He then wants us to share that blessing to the people around us. With that thought in mind, let's look at one more scripture before we go any further. In Matthew 5:14, Jesus states, *"You are the light of the world. A city that is set on a hill cannot be hidden."* So, already, we have seen as Christians that we are called into light and not darkness, we are to be a blessing with what we have, and we are to be a light. Every single one of us needs to take ownership and be empowered to bring light to people who only see darkness! I pray that is exactly what this book will help you do. **We cannot sit idly by and watch our friends and family sink into the dark and lonely pit of anxiety, depression and mental illness without doing everything we can to help.** Before we can help others though, we must get ourselves healthy first.

CHAPTER 1

There are many great aspects of being a pastor. I am so grateful to be called by God into the ministry. In all humility, I truly believe being a pastor is the greatest job in the world! I have never taken for granted the role I play in our church, in our community and in people's lives. Of the many wonderful benefits pastoring includes, helping people is by far the greatest. Whether it is bringing someone into a relationship with the Lord for the first time knowing their eternity is now secure in Heaven, praying for a life-long church member in a time of need, celebrating a milestone or victory with a church member, or giving food and clothing to our community when in need, being a pastor is all about people. If you are not passionate about serving people, you have no business being in the ministry. In my years as a pastor, I have encountered, prayed for and counseled hundreds, if not thousands, of people who are going through a mental or emotional struggle of some variety. I have talked to people who battle occasional anxiety, who have attempted suicide multiple times, who have been medically diagnosed as bipolar or schizophrenic, and everything in between. Like I mentioned before, quite often there seems to be embarrassment and shame associated with the challenges they are facing. Whether consciously or subconsciously, I believe as a society we have accepted a group of misperceptions and lies regarding mental illness. Let's take a look at some of them now.

Misperceptions and lies of mental illness:

 ## Lie 1:
You are alone

This may be the most damaging of all the lies we are going to discuss. This feeling causes us to isolate, to self-medicate, to hide and to feel overwhelmed by what is going on inside us. YOU ARE NOT ALONE! Research shows us that over 60 million Americans are living with some form of mental illness. One in five Americans have taken or are currently taking anti-depressants. Over 40,000 Americans commit suicide annually and over a million attempt it. Again, you are not alone. You are not defeated because of what may be going on inside your head. Some of the greatest names in history, including people in the Bible, had struggles like what you may be dealing with. In Lamentations 3, we see the great Prophet Jeremiah is tormented as he states that his *"soul is far from peace."* In Psalm 18, King David states that *"his soul is in death"* and in Psalm 142, he says that his *"soul is in prison."* Even the great Apostle Paul speaks of himself in 2 Corinthians of being in *"deep despair."* I can tell you that many of the great leaders I know, including myself and my father, have dealt with things like insomnia, severe anxiety, post-traumatic stress disorder (PTSD) and even depression.

Dealing with some sort of mental or emotional challenge is far more common than many will admit, and because of that, there is help – and, nowadays there is far more compassion and understanding than there has been in the past. YOU ARE NOT ALONE! There are plenty of people who want to help. There are countless resources available for you. And most importantly, God loves you and is with you! God's Word is very clear in Hebrews 13:5 that He never leaves you, nor forsakes you. Never means never! Praise God. He is with you in the good times and the bad times. He does not abandon, nor give up on you when life gets hard. God will never give up on you. He will never quit on you. He is always ready and prepared to help you. You may feel alone at times, but you are never alone if you have a relationship with God. In fact, I believe it is during seasons of challenge that we truly see the magnificence and the grace of God when we turn to Him and not away from Him.

 ## Lie 2:
You are weak

I cannot tell you how many people I have spoken to in the past that tried to share their struggles with loved ones around them, only to be told to "get over it" or "just be stronger." Why is it that we have allowed ourselves to believe that any form of mental illness is weakness? We do not say that about any other form of illness. I cannot imagine anyone has ever said "just be stronger" to a family member diagnosed with cancer, lupus or heart disease. It is completely absurd to even imply that we would respond in such a way. A few years ago, a woman in our church came to me to share her diagnosis of rheumatoid arthritis and lupus. My heart broke for her. I was filled with empathy and compassion. We prayed together with her family. I gave her resources and even helped connect her to a couple of specialists for her to get the best medical care we have available in our city. Never once did I think that she should have just been tougher or stronger or that she should simply get past it. The fact that you might be struggling mentally or emotionally right now is not weakness, it is a challenge. Please understand, this is a challenge you must face and walk through – and I pray this book will become part of your healing process.

Please do not believe this lie! You are not weak, and even if you feel weak right now, I believe that you will feel strong once again. Let me share with you one of my favorite passages of scripture. I hope the words will encourage you as you read from 2 Corinthians 12:9-10: *"And He said to me, 'My grace is sufficient for you, for My strength is made perfect in weakness.' Therefore most gladly I will rather boast in my infirmities, that the power of Christ may rest upon me. Therefore I take pleasure in infirmities, in reproaches, in needs, in persecutions, in distresses, for Christ's sake. For when I am weak, then I am strong."* This scripture captivates our minds because it reveals one of God's great intentions toward us: He never leaves us weak. When we are weak, He promises to make us strong. There is a high likelihood you have experienced this before without even knowing it. Have you ever overcome a challenge that you thought you could not have found victory in? We all have! Have you ever gone through a trial that should have destroyed you and, instead, came out stronger on the other end of it? I bet you have. The strength of God is perfected in your weakness. You are not destined for failure and defeat. You are destined for success and victory. You are not weak. You are strong!

 ## Lie 3:
You are hopeless

Too many people who battle depression or any form of mental illness and challenge have been convinced there is no hope for them to get better. Whether through doctors, friends, articles they have read, or just the weight within their own mind of the heaviness they live with, they have accepted that this is a burden they will carry for the rest of their lives. Let me tell you right now, you are not hopeless. You are not defeated. You can overcome this. You do not have to live in a prison of hopelessness, bound to depression and anxiety for the rest of your life. You can have an amazing future. You can be happy once again. You are going to start sleeping through the night with peace and rest. You are not broken beyond repair. You are not damaged goods. There are treatments, natural and supernatural, that work.

Jeremiah 33:6 says, *"Behold, I will bring health and cure. I will heal them and reveal to them the abundance of peace and truth."* God is a healing God. He is the God of health and cure, and I believe there is health and cure for you today. True freedom and peace are found in Jesus, your Lord and Savior. Do you believe it? If you don't, I pray as you read this book that your faith will come alive and be fully energized to expect to be delivered from the dark cloud of pain you have been living under. Just look at the promise of God in the above scripture. He not only wants to bring you peace and truth, but He also wants to reveal it to you in abundance. Maybe you have lived in an abundance of heaviness and pain; going forward you are going to enjoy an abundance of peace! It is the dawn of a new day in your life. Better times are ahead of you. God is good and His healing and restoration is going to work in your life in incredible ways to empower you to live a life you enjoy.

 ## Lie 4:
It is your fault

Unfortunately, humanity can be very hard and lack empathy. We see it on the news, in articles we read, and on social media. Sometimes it feels like everywhere you turn, people are tearing others apart with anger, mocking, judgment and condemnation. It is done under the guise of exposing others so they will change, yet far too often, we are just hurting each other due to a lack of compassion, benefit of the doubt, and understanding. This behavior is so prevalent in our society today that we have coined a term to describe it: "cancel culture." To tell someone who is battling for their peace and joy that it is their fault is such a selfish response. No one would choose depression. People do not wake up one day and decide to have panic attacks. No one wants to live feeling like the world is caving in on them and everyone is against them. I have never met someone who was overjoyed at the lack of sleep they were getting because they were gripped with anxiety all night. This is not your fault! I do not want to live in a cancel culture; I would much rather live in a **counsel** culture where people are inspired to help others and not destroy them.

John 10:10 says, *"The thief does not come except to steal, and to kill, and to destroy."* Mental illness is not your fault. Depression is not your fault. Anxiety is not your fault. The enemy is attacking your life trying to rob you of the life God has for you. And what is that life? The rest of the scripture says, *"I have come that they may have life, and that they may have it more abundantly."* Jesus came for you to have a great life filled with an abundance of joy, peace and happiness.

7

Let's stop believing the lies the world tells us. These lies are not told for our benefit. Rather, they are designed to get us to quit, to resign to depression, and to cause us to feel like we must live a lesser quality of life. The enemy wants you to be bound and held hostage by whatever negativity has overcome you. Can you fight it though? Yes, you absolutely can. Galatians 5:1 in the Message Translation says, *"Christ has set us free to live a free life. So take your stand! Never again let anyone put a harness of slavery on you."* It is not God's plan or desire for you to live in bondage. Jesus came for you to be free. Free from depression. Free from anxiety. Free from suicidal thoughts and tendencies. Free from self-doubt and hate. Free from torment. Jesus wants you to be free! Praise the Lord. We have been gifted the promise of freedom. With that said, did you see what the rest of the scripture says? It says, "so take your stand." It is time to take a stand. It is time for you to fight back. It is time for you to decide that you are going to be free once again. It is time for you to walk into your promise of freedom and live in the fullness of the joy, peace and happiness that Jesus came to give you. In this book, you will learn exactly how to do so.

■ Stop defending and start
1 believing

Because of the lies, misperceptions, lack of knowledge and judgments associated with mental illness and struggle, millions of people live with a sense of shame or embarrassment about what they are dealing with. This is just not right. Let me say that again: It is not right. The time is now to remove the stigma associated with anxiety, depression, PTSD, insomnia, and any other type of mental or emotional challenges our family and friends are living with. It is only at the point the stigma is removed — and we as a society start responding with compassion and empathy — that those struggling will be able to come out of isolation and get the help and support they need. If you are struggling, please do not accept the feeling that you are alone and defeated. Start going to church. Start volunteering. Start praying. Start reading the Bible. Get counseling with a professional counselor or a pastor.

Unfortunately, the negative response many have given in the past has also caused people to be very guarded and defensive about their personal struggle. Let's decide now that instead of defending, we will start believing in the God who heals, delivers and restores. I want to remind you that nothing is impossible to God. He is for you and not against you. He is the God who brings restoration and recovery. There is nothing greater on this earth than His power. You can, and I believe you will, find freedom and joy once again. Do you believe it? I pray you do! What you choose to believe is the first step in taking a stand. Mark 9:23 says, *"If you can believe, all things are possible to Him (Jesus) who believes."* All things are possible to Jesus. He is the Savior, Deliverer and Healer. We just choose to believe. Yes, believing is a choice you make. You decide what you are going to believe and not believe. The reason I encourage you to go to church, pray, get counseling and read your Bible is because Romans 10:17 says, *"So then faith comes by hearing, and hearing by the word of God."* The more you know God, the more your believing will be encouraged and uplifted. Maybe in the past, your faith was pointed in all the wrong directions; let's change that going forward. Get your faith pointed in the God of the impossible.

■ Release your
2 burdens to God

Let me ask you a question: where do you turn when the burdens of life arise? Do you run to God or to the world? The world system is a lie. God is the truth. The world system says it will give you pleasure, peace and satisfaction, but the truth is that it only produces trouble, worry and emptiness. Jesus says in Matthew 11:28-30, *"Come to Me, all you who labor and are heavy laden, and I will give you rest. Take My yoke upon you and learn from Me, for I am gentle and lowly in heart, and you will find rest for your souls. For my yoke is easy and My burden is light."*

Here are a few more questions. Did you know that God loves you? Did you know that He thinks the world of you and wants nothing more than to have a relationship with you that He designed to make your life better? Did you know that God is ready and able to help you? In fact, the Bible says in Psalms 46:1 that *"God is our refuge and our strength, our ever-present help in times of trouble."* Isn't that amazing? God is ready and able to help you. The great disciple named Peter instructed us in 1 Peter 5:7 to cast our cares (anxiety) upon Him, for Jesus cares for us. We are invited to release our cares and burdens to God so He can begin to intervene in our lives to help bring us the solutions we need. God's desire is to turn your mourning into joy, your weeping into rejoicing, your fear into faith, your unforgiveness into mercy, and your bondage into freedom. God is so good and loves you so much that He is there for you when all else fails. When your friends have abandoned you. When your life is turned upside down. When we don't know what to do or where to go. In the best times and in the worst times, God is with you and He is for you! Everything starts with God though. He knows the beginning from the end and the end from the beginning. If you are going to change your life, it starts with Jesus.

9

3 Run to hope

Anxiety and depression will tell you there is no hope for you. It will try to convince you that you are bound to this life of pain and torment. The voice inside your head will scream repeatedly that you are stuck in this life and you will never experience a life of joy and peace. The lie is that you are hopeless, but you are not! Again, you are not hopeless! Did you know that the words hopeless and hopelessness do not even appear in the Bible? Isn't that curious? What that tells us is that there is no hopelessness to God's children. He is the God of hope. Jesus is the hope of humanity. The Bible says we have been given a living hope and that it is the anchor of our souls. Romans 15:13 says, *"Now may the God of hope fill you with all joy and peace in believing, that you may abound in hope by the power of the Holy Spirit."* We see here that joy and peace are directly connected to hope.

Hebrews 6:19 in the Message Translation tells us to *"grab the promised hope with both hands and never let go."* Why? Because hope is a positive expectation of good for your future. There is power in hope. A famous cliché in American English is "with just a glimmer of hope." We tend to ignore or smirk at clichés, yet so often they carry profound truth. It is amazing what hope can do for your life. Just a glimmer of hope can inspire you to try one more time, to forgive one more time, to be generous one more time, to pray one more time, to call one more time, or to study one more time. Even the smallest amount of hope can inspire and produce deep change and lasting impact. Hope has power because hope says life can get better. Hope is the antithesis of anxiety and worry. Hope is inspirational and cannot be overcome. Hope inspires and fulfills our faith and expectation of God and our lives. Don't let go of hope. Don't turn away from it. Run to hope, believing in God's Word that promises: hope in Jesus never disappoints. From this moment forward, your life is going to get better. Be filled with a positive expectation for good things to happen, not only mentally or emotionally, but in every area of your life. As you read this, your natural instinct may be telling you otherwise. Because of the struggles you have or are facing, you may be telling yourself that there is no hope for you, but I believe your outlook will change as you continue to read this book. In the coming chapters, you will learn the step-by-step process God's Word lays out for anyone to apply to their life. This process will empower you to find peace and rest mentally, emotionally and spiritually. God is good, and His goodness is going to be the rule of your life in the years ahead.

11

The Missing Peace

The Missing Peace

I was raised by two incredible parents in a wonderful home. My parents, Charles and Rochelle Nieman, brought my sister and I up to love Jesus, to serve God and to walk by faith. We grew up believing in God's Word and building our lives on it. We were taught from a young age to live our lives in reverence and honor to God, while doing our best to give Him glory through our words and our deeds. We were raised in church, surrounded by God-loving and God-fearing people. In a lot of ways, we were sheltered from the outside world. I do not say that as a criticism. In fact, I am quite grateful for it. My parents showed me what integrity, grace, love and Christianity truly are. They were pastors not just on stage, but in our home as well. They were not different people when the lights were on as when they were off. I grew up being taught the things of God and what it means to build your life trusting in the Lord. I have seen God's hand of provision and grace actively moving in my family and in our church year after year throughout my life.

And yet, as I entered high school and college, I found myself dealing with an internal struggle. When I was 15, I began to question myself. From outside appearances, you would never be able to tell that I was incredibly insecure. I found myself searching, anxious, unhappy and feeling unsettled. I did not even know what I was seeking, but I was searching. Like many teenagers, I began to party. At the point I entered college, I had quit and restarted drinking multiple times, trying not to let myself get out of control. At the same time, I was getting more and more addicted to nicotine. By the time I was 21

13

years old, I was smoking two packs of cigarettes per day. When I turned 40, someone asked what my greatest regret in life was. I responded that I do not believe in living in regret. It is truly one of the most dangerous and damaging human emotions to allow to fester within your soul. I told this person that I am very much a present and future thinker, but I do wish I had never started smoking. The years of battle to overcome it and the damage it causes are just simply not worth it. While in college and beyond, I continued to struggle. I developed incredible anxiety. I found myself having increased trouble sleeping – to the point that I matched the medical description of having insomnia. I grew angry. Angry at myself. Angry at people who seemed so happy. Wrongly angry at God. At one point, I was even angry at my family. There was no justification for the anger, but there I was. I also found myself having bouts of depression. Like millions of others dealing with similar challenges, I never said a word about it to anyone. I bottled it up and tried to deal with it myself. I believed the lies we discussed in chapter one. And how could the pastor's kid, who grew up with such great parents and a great life, have so many issues? I felt like I was all alone. Have you ever felt that way? I bet many of you have.

As I transitioned into marriage and ministry, I discovered I was not at all alone. In fact, I began to realize there is a great Christian frustration. I talked to, prayed for and counseled countless men, women, young adults and teenagers who were searching for something they were missing. On varying levels, they were tormented, anxious, depressed and sometimes suicidal. At one point, I spent two hours every Thursday for ten straight weeks with a man I went to school with whose depression and anger issues resulted in domestic assault and battery charges, firing from his job, and a marriage on the brink of divorce. His life was in ruins. Like me, he was raised in a Christian home. He knew Jesus. He loved God and wanted to serve God; but he was broken. He was hurting. He was living in darkness, convinced he would never see light again. He was desperate for change, and praise God, he found it.

After all the prayer calls, counseling appointments, and personal victories, I realized that the frustration inside countless Christians and others alike is that they are missing peace. So many Christians hear scripture after scripture about the peace of God. We know that Jesus is called the Prince of Peace. We know that on the night Jesus was born, the angel of the Lord declared, "Peace on earth." Yet, for so many, peace is still missing in their lives. Their minds run wild with worry, anxiety and negative thoughts. Their hearts are burdened by disappointment, bitterness and depression. They live feeling like their souls are being torn apart and broken into pieces and have no idea how to put the pieces back together. Therefore, I went on a journey to study what peace is in the Bible. I wanted not only to know what peace was and how to instill it into my life, but also how to teach people around the world to do the same. I believe with all my heart that the next chapters will encourage and empower you into a place of healing and peace within your soul. I have no doubt God will anoint this book and bring thousands and thousands of people into freedom from the dark cloud of mental and emotional turmoil. Is that because I am so smart and such an amazing writer? Absolutely not. It is because God's Word is true. It is relevant. It is uplifting. It is a Word of healing and deliverance. Mostly, it is applicable to our everyday lives and through it, peace will be obtained.

LUKE 2:14

"Glory to God in the highest, and on earth peace, goodwill toward men!"

This is one of the most famous scriptures in the Bible. Most people think about and discuss this scripture annually as they celebrate Christmas with friends, families and loved ones. Of course, this was spoken by the angel of the Lord to mankind on the very night our Lord and Savior, the Messiah, was born. Let's think about this for a second before we go any further. This is a monumental moment in human history. This is the beginning of the destiny of Jesus Christ to come and redeem humanity from its sins. This is the night everything would change, and our Heavenly Father has sent a multitude of angels from Heaven to deliver a message. It is not at all a long message. In fact, it is quite short. With that in mind, we must realize that the message carries immense importance and significance for our lives. This is the moment. This is the night Jesus is born and our Heavenly Father has something to say. Bear in mind, He can say whatever He wants. The angel will deliver any word in any language using any syllable ever created. In fact, God could have created new words, even a new language in this exact moment and given mankind the ability to understand what He wanted to say. This is God. He is not limited to anything or any circumstance. And in this vital moment, the message He has the angel deliver is "peace, goodwill toward men." Peace and goodwill. Not faith. Not love. Not joy. Not mercy, hope, forgiveness or unity. Not any of the other life-changing messages that appear throughout the Bible. None of those things. Our Heavenly Father's message on the night His Son came to fulfill His purpose was one of peace and goodwill toward mankind. That is simply incredible, and I believe it shows that God knows the importance of peace in our lives.

As we begin this journey together, we need to pay very close attention to the wording of this scripture. Notice that God declared peace and goodwill toward men, not amongst men. This is incredibly important. He did not say from the moment Jesus arrived on the earth that there would be peace on earth among men. Clearly, that has not been and is not the case at this very moment. We have had centuries of war and unrest around the world among people and countries. There is evil in the earth and there will never fully be peace among men until eternity is established and Heaven is brought to earth – but there is peace toward men from God. In the literal text, the word **toward** means "will remain in place." What an amazing reality. God is directing peace and goodwill from His throne to His children, and it will remain in place for eternity. There is nothing anything or anyone can do – past, present or future – that can change this God-appointed declaration. **No matter what your life has looked like and no matter what is going on in our world, the attitude and directive of God to you is peace and goodwill.** Praise the Lord! This is something to be excited about. This is something to rejoice about. This is a promise that should give you hope in every moment of your life, for the rest of your life. No matter what is going on, you have peace from God, and this is the starting point to your possession of peace in your heart and mind. This is the reason Jesus came to the earth. Before He came, there was distance, separation and frustration between God and man; but on this night, everything changed. Now, there is no more distance. There is no more separation. There is no more frustration. There is only peace and goodwill. So, that begs this question: When the Bible talks about peace, what does it actually mean?

Peace in the New Testament:

1 Tranquility of your heart and mind arising from reconciliation with God

It should not escape us that the first definition of peace in the New Testament addresses tranquility in our hearts and minds. Right off the bat, God shows that He desires for us to live our lives with mental and emotional peace. He does not want or plan for us to be tormented by anxiety, panic, fear and unrest. The darkness those emotions bring into our souls is not part of the abundant life Jesus came to give us. In fact, Philippians 4:4-6 states, *"Be anxious for nothing, but in everything by prayer and supplication, with thanksgiving, let your requests be made known to God; and the peace of God, which surpasses all understanding, will guard your hearts and minds through Christ Jesus."* What a wonderfully simple, but incredibly encouraging scripture this is. God says to us, instead of worrying and being anxious, come to Me with your concerns and I will deliver you into a place of tranquility.

Peace is attainable for you, and the source of that peace is our reconciliation with God. We see in 2 Corinthians 5 that we have right standing with God because we have been made new in Christ. The scripture is speaking of our salvation in Jesus. As Christians, we are recipients of the greatest gift ever given to mankind: the gift of salvation. God took it upon Himself through Jesus to give us right standing. Right standing with God opens the door for peace to enter your life. You can live free from the guilt, shame and regret of your past knowing that God has forgiven you. Scripture goes on to show us that upon entering into a relationship with the Lord

17

and being set right in the eyes of God the Father, you are made a new creation in Christ Jesus. 2 Corinthians 5:17 in the Message Translation says, *"Anyone united with the Messiah gets a fresh start, is created new. The old life is gone; a new life burgeons."* You can rest peacefully going forward knowing that God is not in Heaven judging you over your past. He is not determining your future based on what you did as a young adult, or even last week. He is planning a great life for you based on His amazing promises and plans that were formulated out of His divine love, not His wrath.

▪ Living with a sense of divine favor
2 with God

Here is where peace begins to become attainable for us and relevant to our daily lives. The absence of peace comes from nervousness, insecurities and feeling overwhelmed by life and circumstance; but that anxiety begins to dissipate when you understand that God is with you in every area of your life to fulfill the wonderful plans He set out for you. Romans 5:17 says, *"For if by the one man's offense death reigned through the one, much more those who receive abundance of grace and of the gift of righteousness will reign in life through the One, Jesus Christ."* Through our relationship with Jesus, we are gifted right standing with God which produces an abundance of grace. His grace is His favor upon our lives, and the scripture says that favor allows us to "reign in life." There is no circumstance or obstacle in your life that is greater than the power of the God you serve. At our church in El Paso, we remind people in every service that Romans 8:31 says that God is on our side. That scripture goes on to reveal to us that because He is on our side, we will not lose; rather, we will have victory. You are called to reign in life. You are given the power and authority by Him to maintain control over yourself and choose to not be ruled by the ways of the world. God is with you. God is for you. God is greater than the enemy.

For many people, this truth is very challenging to wrap their heads around. Bad teaching, religion, and self-imposed judgment has created a perception that God is out to get them. People have been told He may trip them up, strike them down, or even pull His blessing away from their life. These beliefs could not be further from the truth. You have unmerited favor with God. In everything you do, everywhere you go, with every person you come in contact with, God is working on your behalf to make good things happen. Please understand, once and for all, God is always on your side. He is for you and never against you. He wants to open doors for you. He wants everything you set your hand upon to prosper. He wants you to enjoy your life, so you and the people around you will see His good work in and through you. It is time to accept the gift of favor that Jesus died on the cross for you to experience. This reality allows you to walk confidently daily, weekly and annually, knowing the grace of God will empower you into a life of fulfilled dreams, found purpose, and manifested satisfaction. This great reality should give you incredible peace.

▪ 3 Health, welfare, prosperity and every kind of good

In this very moment and for the rest of your life, health, welfare, prosperity and every kind of good is flowing from God to you. Praise the Lord. This definition changed my life. It gives me such hope and builds my faith in so many ways. I pray it will do the same for you. When the stress and burden of life tries to weigh you down, remind yourself that God has good things planned for you. He wants you to prosper, to live well and to be healthy. These promises extend into every area of your life. God wants you to have a healthy mind and body. He wants you to live confidently with joy because your relationships, your finances and your career are prospering. He is not the God of lack; He is the God of provision. God desires to do good for you. Maybe you were raised not to expect much out of life. Maybe you have been overwhelmed by insecurity and doubt. Maybe you have just given up in certain areas of your life. This definition of peace can help reshape your thinking and change the expectation you have for your future. Begin to believe that God is going to deliver unto you health, welfare, prosperity and every kind of good. Why don't you just say it aloud right now? Come on, do it. I know it may feel a bit weird, but you need to start speaking words of life over yourself and your family. Just say, "God, give me health, welfare, prosperity and every kind of good!" Now, say it again. And one more time. Okay, how about one more time, but this time, say it like you believe it. "God, give me health, welfare, prosperity and every kind of good."

Why am I being so repetitive about this? Simple: if you allow this reality of your promise from God to sink into your heart and mind, the entire framework of how you see yourself, how you see your future, and how you see God will be transformed. The transformation will eliminate hopelessness, doubt and fear from your life. One more time, "God, give me health, welfare, prosperity and every kind of good!" Make this part of your daily prayer life. Pray it in times of anxiety, for His peace will mount up and guard your heart and mind. In fact, say it the way you feel it, "God, give me health, welfare, prosperity and every kind of good over the situation I am worried about, in Jesus' name, Amen."

4 God is not mad at you

Romans 5:1 states, *"Therefore, having been justified by faith, we have peace with God through our Lord Jesus Christ."* This is truly an incredible scripture that opens to us an amazing reality we have as God's children, because of what Jesus did on the cross. We are justified by faith through Jesus. The word justified means we have been given the right to proclaim by faith what is ours in Jesus Christ. Our justification allows us access to the promises of God: promises of grace, mercy, joy, healing, deliverance, restoration, recovery and peace. You have been given the right to declare them and walk by faith into the wonderful life Jesus wants you to enjoy.

This is all possible because we have peace with God. When you study the phrase "peace with God" in Romans 5:1, you discover that it means "the end of hostility between God and man." To put it simply, God is not mad at you. How is that even possible? So many of us have sinned. By our own estimates, we have been foolish, reckless and even just not great people. Many have been convinced that God is mad at them. I have spoken to countless people who truly believe that God has punished or will punish them. Many think there is a price to pay to God for their sin. Unfortunately, millions of people believe this way. They carry a burden of shame and fear of God that they do not have to carry. In fact, God does not want you to be burdened at all by your past. That is why Jesus died for our sins. It is time to release that heaviness and live in a new reality of God loving you and wanting to empower you to live an amazing life. The Bible says Jesus paid the price for your sins on the cross at Calvary so you can be forgiven. His blood was shed so yours never will be. He was made a curse so you can be blessed. He was made poor so you can be well supplied. Jesus was rejected so you can be eternally accepted. God poured out His wrath on His Son so you and I can live in peace with Him. He is not mad at you. In fact, He only loves you. He cherishes you. He values you. He thinks the world of you. He wants nothing more than to bring health, welfare, prosperity and every kind of good into your life. And that is why the last words of Jesus on the cross were, *"It is finished."* He paid the price in full for you to have peace with your Heavenly Father.

5 All blessing

Have you ever been reading your Bible and just glanced over scriptures without giving them much thought or attention? I have. If I am telling the full truth and nothing but the truth, I probably do it more than I really care to admit or even realize. I tend to do it at the beginning or end of a chapter when the author is greeting his target audience or closing his thought. In several places in the writings of the Apostle Paul, he closes chapters by saying, *"Now the God of all peace be with you all."* In my study of peace in the Bible, I discovered that every time Paul uses that phrase, the definition of the word "peace" changes. The literal translation of that phrase is, "Now the author and giver of all blessing be with you all." The God of peace is the God of all blessing. God is peace. He is blessing. You cannot separate God from who He is. That is why Jesus is called the Prince of Peace. He is the Prince of tranquility. He is the Prince of favor. He is the Prince of health. He is the Prince of welfare. He is the Prince of prosperity. He is the Prince of every kind of good. He is the Prince of justification. He is the Prince of blessing. And most importantly, the Prince of Peace and all blessing is with you always.

Colossians 3:15 says, *"And let the peace of God rule in your hearts, to which you were called in one body; and be thankful."* You have been called by God into a life of peace. This reality should change your life and reshape how you view yourself, your relationship with God, and your future. You have a calling on your life from God, and that calling is one of peace. With that in mind, let me encourage you that you are now going to begin to walk in your calling. At this very moment, your entire mindset should begin to shift away from the anxiety, worry and hopelessness, and shift toward what God has delivered unto you. Your future with God is one full of tranquility, favor, good things and blessings being poured out onto your life. Now is the time to start believing again, to start hoping again, and to start being encouraged that your future is going to be better than your past. You are going to find the peace that has been missing for far too long. You are called by God to live this amazing, peace-filled life. You are going to be happy. You are going to get rest. You are going to sleep again. You are going to have fulfillment and satisfaction in your heart and mind. You are going to live a life of peace. That is your calling and your destiny.

Battle for Your Soul

Battle for Your Soul

From where your life sits today, your future is full of potential and opportunity. Are you excited about the days ahead? Do you feel a sense of wonder and expectation for the years to come? Or has the darkness and pain of your past robbed you of your desire to pursue your calling of peace?

In the coming pages of this book, we will explore how to overcome the attack Satan brings against our lives on a daily basis in an attempt to pollute our souls, disintegrate our hope, weaken our faith and steal our peace. Please take note of the wording in 1 Peter 5:8 which states that our enemy, the devil, goes around like a roaring lion, seeking whom he may devour. The devil is described as a mirage trying to confuse you. He is "like" a roaring lion. But, he is not a lion. The lion is the king of his domain. A lion is powerful, strong, intimidating and aggressive. A lion will fight to protect and feed its family. A lion does not live in fear of other animals. Quite the contrary, lions instill fear into those around them. And that is why the devil wants us to perceive him as a lion – but he is not. He does not have power over you. He cannot control you. He cannot defeat you. He cannot overcome you, unless you let him. Notice the scripture states, "seeking whom he may devour." It does not state, "seeking whom he can devour." Do you remember raising your hand in grammar school to ask the teacher, "Can I go to the restroom?" only to be corrected with a response similar to the following statement, "Of course you can go to the restroom, but you may not until I give you permission." That used to frustrate me so much. It honestly made me want to scream. Of course, I didn't,

"I pray that you may prosper in all things and be in health, just as your soul prospers."

because I was rightfully taught to respect and honor my teachers at all times, including when I was not happy with what was going on or when I disagreed with something they had told me to do or not do. In hindsight, I am incredibly grateful for that lesson I was taught: 'may I' is all about permission being granted, while 'can I' is all about ability. The great disciple Peter wrote that the devil seeks whom he MAY devour, not whom he CAN devour, to teach us that we must grant the enemy permission to devour us, to destroy us, and to pollute our lives. My response to this truth is, "Satan, no you may not!" This should be your exact response as well.

Please understand, there is a daily battle taking place for rule of your soul. God wants you to place Him as Lord over it to fill you with love, joy, happiness and peace. The enemy wants to steal that from you and fill you with bitterness, sadness, disappointment and anxiety. You must determine to win this battle no matter what it takes. We cannot allow the enemy to gain control of our souls, our hearts and our minds. When Jesus rose from the grave after being crucified, He rose with victory in His hands for His children. The Word of God clearly states time and again that your enemy has been rendered powerless over your life. You must decide to not allow yourself to be deceived into believing that he is a powerful lion that cannot be stopped; believing that lie would grant him permission to rob you of the calling of peace God promised you. You can do this. God is on your side and greater is He who is in you than he who is in the world.

The condition of your soul will determine what dominates your life, placing incredible importance on taking control of it and not allowing the enemy to rule it. 3 John 1:2 says, *"I pray that you may prosper in all things and be in health, just as your soul prospers."* God wants your life to prosper in every area, and much of that prosperity and health will be determined by the condition of your soul. After learning the definition of peace is health, welfare, prosperity and every kind of good, you can now see that 3 John is saying that a prosperous soul is directly connected to peace in your life. You cannot underestimate the value and importance of a healthy soul. Your soul is who you are. It is the combination of what is in your heart and mind. It is your predominant thoughts, your passions, your beliefs, your convictions, your dreams and your desires. Your soul is what defines you as a person. Your soul determines how you see the world, how you respond to opportunities and pressure, and how you view the future. As your soul goes, so goes your life.

What is the condition of your soul? Is your heart in a good place right now? What is in your mind? Are you thinking the thoughts of God, or is your mind filled with negativity and fret? As humans, it is entirely our responsibility to guard our hearts and discipline our minds to function the way God wants them to function. In fact, He has empowered each one of us to take control of our souls and build health and wellness into our hearts and minds, no matter what is going on in our lives or in society. We all have and will continue to experience difficulties and challenges in life. The world has plenty of problems. We also make bad decisions that result in consequences we did not plan and do not enjoy. Sometimes other people's behavior negatively affects us or our families. In John 16:33, Jesus makes this incredible statement: *"These things I have spoken to you, that in Me you may have peace. In the world you will have trouble (distress and suffering); but be of good cheer, I have overcome the world."* Trouble comes in all shapes and sizes. Trouble can come and go quickly, and sometimes it can linger. Maybe you feel like you are stuck in a season of distress and suffering, but you must turn your focus to what Jesus has said about your life and your situation. **He is fully aware of the fact that you will experience difficulties, pain and hardships in life, but He has spoken life into those seasons. He has declared that even in the worst of situations, you can still have peace.** This is possible because you live in faith, knowing that Jesus has overcome the trouble of the world – and because He has overcome, you too shall overcome. Please notice now, Jesus says, "Be of good cheer." That is the part we play in this promise.

27

He delivered peace. He overcame the world. Now, we must choose to be of good cheer, to have peace and to be confident that we live with God's divine favor abounding toward us in every situation.

Trouble comes to limit your life. The enemy wants you to feel overwhelmed by the size of the challenge or the length of the difficult season. The defining issue of your life will not be what happens to you, but rather how you respond to it. Will you be overcome by life or will you be an overcomer? That is a decision you make within your soul. **You cannot be victorious with a victim's mentality.** I am fully aware I will never be able to comprehend or understand the depth and scope of the pain many of you have been through. Some of you have experienced tragedy in your families. Some of you were raised in situations where evil abounded and you were abused mentally, emotionally or physically. Some of you have experienced financial devastation due to the greed of your employers, bad decisions or even a global pandemic. Trouble will come soon enough, and that is why it takes absolute commitment to win the battle of your soul and live a peaceful and prosperous life. Your future should not be ruled or determined by the events of your past, regardless of how terrible they were. Your future is not defined by what happened to you, but rather by what is happening inside you. To be of good cheer in the original text of the Bible also carries with it the definition *"to have courage."* In any fight, whether mental, emotional, physical or natural, courage will be required to win the fight. The so-called lion, Satan, wants to scare you into defeat, because he knows there's no other way. It may be fear alone that's keeping you from the life you want, and the life God wants for you. "Have courage," Jesus said, He is going to deliver you from trouble. The choice of courage, even small, can be scary; but, it will produce great reward. Allow yourself to have enough courage and faith to believe that you are going to get better. Give yourself permission to dream about a day where you are not depressed or miserable any longer. Take a step of faith today. Does it feel risky? Most likely, but nothing incredible ever happened without taking a little risk. It is far riskier to continue to live with a tormented soul that will drag you into a black hole of darkness. Standing between you and your peace is the choice of courage. Be strong and courageous. Stand firm in your faith knowing that you shall overcome.

Fostering A Prosperous Soul:

In Psalms 142, King David writes a prayer in memory of the days he was being persecuted by King Saul. David had slain the great giant named Goliath and won the affection of the people inside the King's courts. Not to mention, David had already been anointed the future king of Israel by the prophet Samuel. Saul grew angry and jealous of the adoration David was receiving. What he should have done was control his emotions, embrace David, and mentor him in a manner that would have set David up for great success over the kingdom they both dearly loved. For quite some time, Saul set out to kill David. Talk about trouble coming into your life. From one moment to the next, David went from being the hero and future king to running for his life and hiding in the shadows from the most powerful man in the region. Of course, David dwelled in God's protection and Saul never accomplished what he set out to do. In this passage, David recounts crying out to the Lord while hiding in a cave, running for his very life and simply trying to survive. When you read this Psalm, there is no other conclusion you can make other than to say that David was in a state of depression, and is desperate to get out of it. Please read the entire Psalm and then I will break it down for you to show you how to win the battle for your soul while simultaneously fostering prosperity within it.

29

(1) *"I cry out to the Lord with my voice; with my voice to the Lord I make my supplication."*

(2) *"I pour out my complaint before Him; I declare before Him my trouble."*

(3) *"When my spirit was overwhelmed within me, then You knew my path. In the way in which I walk they have secretly set a snare for me."*

(4) *"Look on my right hand and see, for there is no one who acknowledges me; refuge has failed me; no one cares for my soul."*

(5) *"I cried out to You, O Lord: I said, 'You are my refuge, my portion in the land of the living.'"*

(6) *Attend to my cry, for I am brought very low; deliver me from my persecutors, for they are stronger than I."*

(7) *"Bring my soul out of prison, that I may praise Your name; the righteous shall surround me, for You shall deal bountifully with me."*

This is an incredible set of scriptures. What a roller coaster of emotion, passion, desperation and need we see from David during this prayer. David is clearly exhausted on every level. He is worn out and overwhelmed by the situation he has found himself in. He is supposed to be learning how to be King of Israel, enjoying marriage, starting a family, and maturing as a man and future leader. He is not supposed to be hiding in the shadows for fear of his life. Sometimes life takes turns we did not expect. Situations happen and profoundly affect you in a negative manner. As overwhelming as circumstances may be, God is greater. Nothing is bigger than Him. No situation is too hard for your Savior. David is so depressed in this cave that he feels his soul is in a prison. He is bound and captive to the state he is in, but he also knows he can get out of it. If David can do it, so can you.

30

Here is how:

■ Cry Out to
1 God in Prayer

Psalms 142 is not the only scripture King David is in or recalls a troubling situation in his life, some of which he created by his wrongdoing. No matter the situation, no matter the challenge, and no matter whose fault it was, David always knew to cry out to God in prayer. The Bible consistently teaches us to "pray without ceasing." In all things, God tells us to pray. In any situation, good or bad, happy or sad, easy or difficult, God is waiting to hear from you; yet, too many people stay silent.

You are always invited by God to go to Him for help. He is ready and waiting for you to go to Him with your worries, your complaints, your troubles, your concerns, your dreams, your desires and any other emotion that is within you. In fact, Hebrews 4:16 says to come boldly to the throne of grace, to obtain mercy and find grace (favor) to help in times of need. Where do you run in time of need? Who do you turn to when trouble comes? Do you run to God or do you run away from God? Psalm 34:17 says, *"The righteous cry out, and the Lord hears, and delivers them out of all their troubles."* That is exactly what David did while his soul was in prison, hiding in a cave. He cried out to God and the Lord delivered him from his physical enemy, King Saul, and his emotional enemy as well.

I truly believe prayer is underutilized in the fight for peace. Society has devalued it through religion and misinformation. On too many occasions and for far too long, prayer has been trivialized, complicated, turned into a formula, and used as punishment. For millions of Christians, prayer has become vain repetition, boring and a dreaded duty. But that is not what prayer is meant to be. Prayer is a God-given gift to go to Him on demand and access His grace, mercy and peace. Just do not run away from God in times of need; run to Him and His favor will be empowered over your life to meet your need. Prayer is a conversation with God where you can talk, listen, praise, complain and ask for wisdom from Him. You do not have to complicate prayer. Talking to God is the same as talking to a friend, just with better results. Prayer gives you access to all God has in store for you through your relationship with Jesus. Prayer is not meant to be begrudged, rather it is meant to be something to be excited about because of what God does for you when you pray.

31

Jesus himself said in Matthew 7:7–8, *"Ask, and it will be given to you; seek, and you will find; knock, and it will be opened to you. For everyone who asks receives, and he who seeks finds, and to him who knocks it will be opened."*

■ Do Not Get
2 Overwhelmed

Obviously, this is easier said than done. We have all felt overwhelmed on numerous occasions in our lives. I remember how overwhelmed

I felt the afternoon my wife and I drove our first-born son home from the hospital. I remember how overwhelmed I felt the first time I preached at our church. I remember how overwhelmed I felt when my mother passed away from stage four ovarian cancer in 2012. I remember how overwhelmed I felt during the COVID-19 pandemic when our church was shut down for three months. I remember how overwhelmed I felt when our church reopened only to have around 20 percent of our church family return to in person services. I remember how overwhelmed I felt as I was airlifted to Florida to have an emergency back surgery after my fifth back surgery had failed. Yes, I have had six back surgeries. Being overwhelmed is a part of life, but you must face it and not to allow it to put your soul into captivity of darkness.

Staying overwhelmed will never produce a healthy soul or deliver peace into your life. Look again at David's words in verses 3 and 4 of Psalm 142:

> *"They have secretly set a snare for me"*
> – He is paranoid.
>
> *"There is no one who acknowledges me"*
> – He feels alone and unappreciated.
>
> *"Refuge has failed me"*
> – He feels lost and abandoned.
>
> *"No one cares for my soul"*
> – He is deceived.

These emotions are the consequences of allowing a sense of being overwhelmed to linger in your soul for too long. Quite often, they are a result of fear. I saw an acronym years ago that said fear is "False Evidence Appearing Real." Fear will cause you to overestimate the difficulty and underestimate your ability to overcome it. That is exactly what you see with David in the above situation; his fear has produced unhealthy thinking and feeling. Yet, he shows us the answer in verse 3 when he says, *"When my spirit was overwhelmed within me, then You knew my path."* Again, where do you turn when trouble comes? Jesus is the way, the truth and the life. He is your source and your supply. He can make a way where there seems to be no way. In the book of Isaiah, God speaks of making roads for us through the wilderness and rivers through the desert. If you turn to God, He will direct your steps, show you the right path to walk on, deliver you from your enemies, provide for you in times of need, and never leave your soul imprisoned.

PROVERBS 3:5-6

"Trust in the Lord with all your heart and lean not on your own understanding.

3 Trust God, Trust God, Trust God

I have always been fascinated with Psalms 142. It is a dichotomy of ups and downs and emotional changes from scripture to scripture. David says in verse 4, "refuge has failed me" and immediately in verse 5 he says to God, *"You are my refuge."* In this moment we see what trusting in yourself and others does to you in contrast to what trusting in God does for you. Trusting in others always has the potential to lead to disappointment, frustration or even betrayal; but, trusting in God carries none of those concerns. God does not fail us. He does not disappoint us. He watches over His Word to perform it in our lives. The gospel of grace and peace is given to us packed with over 7,000 promises, all of which are designed to make our lives better. He is the God of peace, favor and good things. He is the Lord of all blessing, and His goodness does not abandon or fail us when trouble arises. He never leaves or forsakes you, and that includes in the worst moments and seasons of life. The question is, who do you trust? Do you trust yourself over God? Do you trust politicians over God? Do you trust your friends and family over God? Or, do you trust God above all?

Proverbs 3:5-6 says, *"Trust in the Lord with all your heart and lean not on your own understanding. In all your ways acknowledge Him, and He will direct your paths."* The moment David puts his trust in God, he begins to come out of His depression. Read what he says again in Psalm 142, verses 5-7:

> *"You are my refuge"*
> – I put my trust in You.
>
> *"My portion in the land of the living"*
> – You are my source and my supply.
>
> *"Attend to my cry, For I am brought very low"*
> – You give me strength when I am weak.
>
> *"Deliver me from my persecutors"*
> – You are my Savior.
>
> *"Bring my soul out of prison"*
> – Deliver me from depression.

34

Unlike in verses 3 and 4, when David's emotions are filled with despair and desperation due to being overwhelmed, he is now seeing clearly, regrouping his strength and finding direction in the Lord. As difficult as it may be when despair attacks your soul, you must trust Jesus will help you endure that season and overcome it through His strength and His promise of peace in your life. Put your trust not in man, but in Him!

4 Remember His Promise

It took seven verses for David to remind himself of the promises of God for his life. In fact, we see it in the last statement of this great Psalm when he says, *"For You shall deal bountifully with me."* Why is it so hard to remember the promises of God when life gets difficult? I think it is simply human nature. We tend to focus on what is wrong, on the pain, the hurt or the size of the obstacle in our way. It takes discipline and intentionality to remember to focus on who God is for us and what He is doing on our behalf, especially in the worst of times. I wonder if David would have avoided a lot of the emotional pain he suffered had he declared God's faithfulness and provision over his life immediately in this situation?

The Word of God tells us in 2 Corinthians that all the promises of God in Him are YES and in Him are AMEN. I pray you will never forget the promises of peace for your life. I encourage you to declare daily over your life that health, welfare, prosperity and every kind of good is coming toward you and your family. Always remember God is your salvation. He is your source and your strength. He is your refuge and your fortress. In Him, your soul can find peace and rest. We must determine within our souls God is faithful, and He will never let us down. Your soul is meant to prosper, and when your soul prospers so too does your life. Do not be shaken by what is going on around you or even within you, and never let yourself forget God's promises. My prayer for you is that your soul will be filled with expectation and excitement for what is to come in your future. I believe your best days are ahead of you. You are going to witness the hand of God move in your life as you turn to Him to restore your peace, joy, strength, favor and freedom in Jesus' name. Your soul shall not be left in prison; your soul shall be free.

35

Guarding Your Heart

Guarding Your Heart

May 4, 2007 was one of the best days of my life. I was almost 28 years old and was getting married to the love of my life, Karla. She is a spectacular woman of God. I am truly blessed by God that He brought her into my life. Truthfully, she entered my life at just the right moment. In my mid-20s, I had begun to work in our church in El Paso, Texas called Abundant Living Faith Center – we have since renamed it to Abundant Church! My mother, another amazing woman of God, had a hint of the struggles I had been dealing with as a young man. She offered me a job when I graduated from Texas State University in the summer of 2002. I honestly believe my mom thought if she could just get me back around her, my father and our church, that God would help me get my life together. I had been a partier. I was addicted to smoking cigarettes. I was struggling with self-doubt, mild depression and insomnia. Throughout college, I really did not have much of a relationship with God. At the time Karla and I began dating, I was finally trying to get control of my life. I wanted to overcome the struggles. For the first time in my life, I had a sincere desire to get closer to God. I was beginning to accept my calling as a leader in the body of Christ. I was completely in love with Karla and wanted to do whatever it took to have an amazing marriage and future together. I woke up on my wedding day and my heart was filled with excitement. I had never experienced anything like the way I felt that day. The Psalmist in chapter 45 makes the statement of a groom on his wedding day, *"My heart is overflowing with a good theme."* That is exactly how I felt that morning. It is also the day I quit smoking, which made for an interesting honeymoon.

Fast forward to September 2010. Karla was pregnant with our first child. Excitement once again filled the air. My mom was buying gifts for a baby without any of us knowing gender yet. We were ordering parenting books online, looking at paint colors for the nursery, and speculating about what color eyes the baby would have. We told the church the big news. Everyone was elated, but it would not stay that way for long. On a day I will never forget, Karla and I went to her doctor for a checkup and a sonogram. It was not good. I remember seeing the doctor's face as she searched and searched for our baby's heartbeat. She changed positions and searched on the other side of Karla's belly, over and over again, to no avail. Sure enough, we had a miscarriage and Karla needed to have a procedure done to remove the tissue from her body because it did not flush out naturally. My heart sank. Karla wept. I called my dad as we left the appointment and he was overcome with sadness. We were heartbroken. All the excitement and jubilation was suddenly replaced with grief and disappointment. We were crushed. I will never forget how helpless I felt as a husband that evening when Karla and I got home. To that point in my life, I had never felt emotional pain like that.

It is truly amazing how life can change from one moment to the next. It never ceases to amaze me how we can be moving along, building our lives, minding our own business, and BANG, everything changes. I believe moments like these are some of the most pivotal and important moments of your life – not because of what happened to you, but because of what happens inside you. Maybe you experienced a tragedy in your family. Maybe your business failed. Maybe your trust was broken and you were betrayed. Maybe you got wrongfully laid off or terminated from a job you were passionate about. Maybe a series of smaller events have combined to create intense pain in your life. Maybe you are simply not happy with who you are and where your life sits right now. No matter what you have gone through or how deep the pain in your heart is, there is an answer. Proverbs 4:23 says, *"Guard your heart with all diligence. For out of it spring the issues of life."* This revelation is important. From your heart comes the issues, the controlling factors and the boundaries of your life. And yet, it is your job to guard your heart. God will not guard your heart for you; only you can do that. In fact, the scripture says to do so with all diligence. What that says to me is that I need to protect the matters of my heart every day of my life. I must be completely intentional about the issues that are allowed to permeate me. **In the good times, in the bad times, in the seasons of joy, in the seasons of hurt, and everywhere in between, I need to control what I allow to become the rule of my heart.** I need to be completely focused and purposeful about allowing the right things into my heart and getting the wrong things out. This verse exposes a great truth for all of us: life is not defined by what happens to you, life is defined by what happens inside of you. On the evening we lost our baby, I drove to a pharmacy near my house to pick up medicine for Karla. As I headed home, I felt so much anger and devastation in my heart, but I also remember knowing I could not allow those emotions to rule me, to overcome my soul. In that very moment, I began to guard my heart. How you respond in your heart will determine your future peace and happiness, particularly in the times or seasons that did not work out the way you intended for them to work out.

Every person alive today will experience hardship and pain. There is sin on the earth. There is turmoil in people. As Christians, we know that we have an adversary who wants to rob us of the abundant life Jesus came to give us. One of the most effective ways Satan robs you of an incredible, peace-filled life is by polluting your heart. He aims to poison you with hurt, discouragement, disappointment and failure. He wants you to give up on life, give up on yourself, and give up on God. The enemy wants you to give into the hurt and pain of your past. He wants you to quit. He wants you to believe in your heart that you will always be depressed, always be broken, and always be hurting. He wants you to accept a life of failure and defeat. Please hear me, you cannot let him have his way with you. You must fight back and take control of your heart, and you can do so with the gift of peace.

Philippians 4:6-7 — *"Be anxious for nothing, but in everything by prayer and supplication, with thanksgiving, let your requests be made known to God; and the peace of God, which surpasses all understanding, will guard your hearts and minds through Christ Jesus."*

The fourth chapter of Philippians is truly one of the greatest chapters of the Bible. I know as a pastor I am not supposed to play favorites with God's Word, but this is my favorite chapter. Some of the greatest scriptures of truth appear in these verses. Of course, many of you know verse 13 that says, *"I can do all things through Christ who strengthens me."* If God said you can do all things, that means you can have a life of peace. Of course, there is also verse 19 that shows the provision and resource of God: *"And my God shall supply all your need according to His riches in glory by Christ Jesus."* He is the God of provision, and we have already seen that God promises us health, welfare, prosperity and every kind of good for our lives. Knowing this, we can only conclude that God is and always will be moving in our lives to fulfill our needs. You cannot live a life of prosperity and lack at the same time. Those conditions do not function in harmony in a person's life. You are either prospering mentally, emotionally, relationally, physically and financially, or you are not. It really is as simple as that, and the God you serve sent Jesus to deliver His peace, provision and blessing into your life.

In the previous chapters, I showed you that the peace of God is His gift to us as His children. Verse 7 in Philippians chapter 4 reveals peace is not only a gift from God, but also a weapon to be used to *"guard our hearts and minds through Christ Jesus."* When you study the word "guard" in the original text, it implies it is a military term used in battle. Isn't that interesting? The peace of God is part of our God-given arsenal to use to overcome the attack of the enemy on our souls, and it is fueled by the power of Jesus Christ. In fact, it is so powerful that the scripture says it *"surpasses all understanding."*

In July 2020, during the COVID-19 stay-at-home orders, Karla and I needed to have some paint repairs done at our house. The owner of the company showed up at 7:00 on a Monday morning. I greeted him and his crew and showed them the minor issues that needed to be addressed. Then, I walked into my home office and began to type chapter 1 of this very book. I was nervous about it and not even sure if I should do it. I am not a writer. I am not a world-renowned speaker or a New York Times #1 bestselling author. As I began to type, the owner of the company came into the office to address an issue in that room. After finishing the repairs and touch-ups, he looked at me said, "I have to thank you.

You saved my life. I went to your church a couple years ago and it happened to be the first Sunday you taught a series called The Missing Peace. I was broken, depressed and not wanting to live anymore, but that series pulled me out of it. I now own my own business and I am happier and more successful than I have ever been. I am not depressed anymore." Clearly, I did not save His life, God's Word did. But in that moment, I knew I had to write this book. Was that a coincidence? No, it was not. I believe God ordained that moment to encourage me and remind me of the very promise I was writing about. He sent that man to help guard my heart and bring me peace as I started to write a book about peace. Isn't God amazing? That is God working beyond understanding.

I believe that depression, anxiety, overburden and any other types of bondage are attacks brought against us by the enemy to destroy our lives. Let me remind you that Jesus has overcome every principality and power of the wicked one, and because Jesus overcame them, you too can overcome them. You can be free from depression. You can overcome those panic attacks. You will have peace and rest once again, or maybe even for the first time. YOU CAN DO ALL THINGS THROUGH JESUS CHRIST. God did not birth you onto this earth to live in bondage. Jesus came with freedom in His hands to give to each and every one of His children. That includes you. You are free! Free from the curse of sin and death. Free from the power of the enemy. Free from bondage and turmoil. Free from depression and oppression. You are free because Jesus has set you free! That freedom is what empowers His peace to guard your heart.

ROMANS 4:18

"...against all hope, in hope Abraham believed"

Some of you may be skeptical as you read this. Maybe you are thinking this only works for some people. You can be skeptical, but my hope is that even in your skepticism, you will begin to believe. From time to time though, you simply must choose to believe something new. For too long you may have believed the exact opposite of what I am telling you, and it has not gotten you anywhere you want to be. Why don't you try believing something different? When God told Abraham, the father of faith, that he would have a child with his barren wife, Sarah, the Bible says *"against all hope, in hope Abraham believed"* (Romans 4:18). I pray as you read this book, a sense of calm and hope will begin to come into your soul, and you will start to experience the life-altering gift of peace God has given you. Now, in that believing, you must determine you will take the necessary steps to guard your heart. Your heart determines the issues of your life. Let me show you how to do just that.

Guarding Your Heart:

1 In Everything, Pray!

Just like we saw in the previous chapter with King David, we see in Philippians that prayer is the first thing we should be doing for our mental and emotional health.

Philippians 4:6-7 — *"Be anxious for nothing, but in everything by prayer and supplication, with thanksgiving, let your requests be made known to God."*

In everything, pray! When you are anxious, pray. When you are nervous, pray. When you are overwhelmed, pray. When you are stressed, pray. When you are facing a serious challenge in life, pray. When you have really messed up, pray. When you have no idea what to do, pray. IN EVERYTHING, PRAY. Isn't it incredible that God tells us to go to Him even in our worst moments? The problem is that typically, we do not want to. It is not our nature to want to pray when we are feeling anxious, and that is where the battle starts. You must discipline yourself to overcome how you feel in order to do what you need to do. Need must overcome want if you desire to have a great life.

I used to dislike this scripture. Ironically, it caused me anxiety. It stressed me out. I felt as if it was setting me up for failure. I was already battling anxiety and yet it tells me to "be anxious for nothing."

I simply could not fathom the simplicity of this scripture coming to fruition in my life, but it did. As I drove home on the night we had the miscarriage, the realization of the necessity to guard my heart came to me while I was praying. My entire mood began to shift as I prayed. My anger diminished. I regained perspective in the knowledge that Karla and I were young, and we had plenty of time to try to start a family once again. Prayer changes things. God does not set us up for failure; He sets us up for success. If we could not do something that He is asking us to do, He would not have included it in His Word. Of course, I did not focus on the solution, only on the problem. So, one day, I challenged myself to pray every time I began to feel anxiety, worry or trouble coming into my heart and mind. Lo and behold, it started to work! The power and importance of prayer can never be underestimated in your life. I pray all the time now. Truthfully, I am not one who typically prays for long periods of time, but I pray a lot. Are they long, deep prayers? Sometimes, but usually not. Just like talking to a friend, not everything requires hours to discuss. The same is true in prayer. I give my concerns and my burdens to God. I find that reminding myself of God's power during prayer builds my spirit and settles my soul. Prayer is the starting point in your life to winning the battle of your soul and guarding your heart.

43

Jesus tells us in the book of Matthew to pursue Him first in every area of our lives and He will provide what we need. In a world full of options, choose Jesus. It is as simple as that. Choose Him. The world is constantly changing, bringing pressure and causing chaos, but you can always rely on His peace to provide for you no matter what is going on around you. The challenging part is reminding ourselves to seek Him first in prayer when we do not feel like it or want to. Prayer is a divine gift from God. It is time to utilize it.

2 Be Specific

God has blessed Karla and me with two wonderful children, Caleb and Charlotte. They are vibrant, smart and full of joy and laughter. As I write this book, Caleb is 8 years old and Charlotte is 5. Needless to say, they are still at the age where they need me or their mother to help them with most things in their lives. We are teaching them to be independent thinkers, with thought processes that identify and solve problems; but, they are still just young children. All day, every day, they come to us when they are hungry, when they are hurt, or when they are confused. They do not hesitate to ask a question or tell us what they need, and trust me, they are specific with what they want. I am sure I am not the only parent with children like this. The thing is, I am happy when they come to me. I want to help them. I want to answer their questions. I am here to provide for their needs. My primary role as their father is to direct their steps on a Godly path of wisdom, integrity and love. We are taught in Philippians to *"let your requests be made known to God and the peace of God will guard your heart."* How? Because His peace is provision. His peace was given to you to provide health, welfare, prosperity and every kind of good. His peace is His blessing. Jesus Himself said to us in Matthew 7:7, *"Ask and you shall receive. Seek and you shall find."*

So, are you asking? Are you seeking? Or are you hesitating? Too many Christians have convinced themselves of the lie that they are bothering God. Just like my children are not bothering me, you are not bothering Him. Jesus said He is our ever-present help in our time of need. He cannot help, though, if we refuse to go to Him. In fact, Matthew 7:11 says, *"If you then, being evil, know how to give good gifts to your children, how much more will your Father who is in heaven give good things to those who ask Him!"*

Here are some very common questions I receive when I teach about this topic, along with the answers I give:

How long do you pray? Until peace comes.
How many times do you pray? As many times as it takes.
How many times do you ask? Until I receive the answer.
How often do you seek? Until I find.
How often do you cry out to God? Every time I am hurting.
Can I ask God anything? Absolutely and without hesitation.
What prayers does God answer? All of them, but He only answers according to His Word.

Please do not hesitate to go to God at any moment of your life, but particularly when anxiety, worry or fear are abounding in your heart. He is there for you and He will never leave or forsake you. He is eagerly waiting to help you and to pour out His peace onto your life.

3 Praise God

We have already seen in Philippians chapter 4 that part of prayer should include praise to God when it said in verse 6, *"Be anxious for nothing, but in everything by prayer and supplication, with thanksgiving, let your requests be made known to God."* The key phrase here is "with thanksgiving." Anxiety and depression will try to convince you that everything in your life is falling apart. Your heart will abound in fear, disappointment and even hatred of yourself or others to the point of hopelessness, self-loathing and a sense of defeat. You will convince yourself you have nothing to live for and no reason to move forward. This is all a design of the enemy to separate you from God, your source of peace, and to get you to lose perspective in life. When we begin to feel this way, we tend to focus only on what is going wrong. We completely lose sight of all the good in our lives. We forget about the God we serve. We diminish the importance and value of our family and friends who love and support us, and only focus on the people who hurt us or are against us. We often lose sight of everything God has given to us and done for us. The enemy is simply trying to turn us away from one of the most powerful aspects of our relationship with God – thanksgiving and praise.

A lot people think that praising God is part of the worship experience during church – you know, the fast songs that are fun and exciting. I love those songs. They energize me and excite me. They also set the tone in my heart for worship, prayer and the teaching of God's Word in His house! I love praising God in a corporate environment, but that is just one aspect of what praise really is. If praise and thanksgiving are part of accessing the peace of God which surpasses understanding, clearly it must extend beyond a weekly church service and there must be power within it.

The first thing we need to understand about praising God is He designed it for us, not for Him. He does not need our admiration.

He is God. He knows far better than we do how glorious, majestic and powerful He truly is. He is not insecure and never wakes up on the wrong side of the bed. He does not need our compliments and encouragement. He is the living God who exists to give you eternity and the abundant life of peace. Praising Him is one way you access it.

Psalm 8:2 — *"Out of the mouths of babes and nursing infants, You have ordained strength because of Your enemies, that You may silence the enemy and the avenger."*

We see in this scripture that God has given us the strength we need to face our enemies. Our God-given strength is so powerful that it carries the ability to silence the enemy and the avenger. In Matthew 21:16, Jesus quotes Psalm 8:2, but we see a slight change in the wording. He says, *"Out of the mouths of babes and nursing infants You have perfected praise."* Our Father has created praise as a weapon to be used against the attack of the enemy in our lives. A small amount of word study shows us that the literal definition of the word praise is "to be strengthened inwardly." The moment you begin to use your words to praise God, whether in a church environment or in prayer by yourself, God begins to strengthen you from the inside out. I cannot tell you how many times I have had people tell me how amazing they feel during praise and worship at church. Is that an accident? Absolutely not. Praising God was created to turn your weakness into strength. In fact, so much of the power in praising God is simply in taking your eyes off the problem and putting them onto the solution as you remind yourself of God's power and authority. We praise God and see His wisdom over our confusion. We are reminded of our hope in Him as a replacement of the anxiety within our souls. I mentioned before that we often lose perspective when we are struggling emotionally and mentally. Praise affords you the ability to regain the proper perspective, a Godly perspective.

Let's take this one step further. Psalm 22:3 shows us God inhabits the praises of His people. Is that not just incredible? He inhabits your praises. When you begin to praise God for who He is and what He does for your life, you are immediately placed within His presence. Remember, where His presence is, there is fullness of love, joy, wisdom and peace. Where His presence is, the presence of the enemy cannot be. Satan cannot occupy the same space as God. When you praise God, Satan is left out of your life. That is why you feel so good when you praise God. That is why you are so encouraged when you are praising Him. That is why you have clarity when you pray. I implore you to live a life of prayer and praise to God. I start every prayer with praising God. I do that to get my mind in the right place and to invite His strength and presence into my life every time I go to Him in prayer. I encourage you to do the same.

Let me give you some practical examples of how to praise God in your prayer time:

God, I praise and thank You that I am forgiven of my sins and set free from shame and regret.

God, I praise You that You are more than enough for me.

God, I thank You that You are greater than any challenge, burden or obstacle that is in my way.

God, I worship You for who You are and what You do. You are holy and wonderful, and I invite Your presence into my heart and mind.

God, I praise You that Your wisdom is being poured out onto my life to lead and guide me.

God, I praise You that no weapon formed against me and my family will prosper and any tongue that rises against us in judgment will be condemned and proven to be in the wrong.

God, I thank You that Your perfect love casts out all my fears.

God, I thank You for giving me a hope and a future filled with good things taking place in my life.

God, I thank You that You are always on my side, and with You on my side, I shall not lose.

God, I praise You for Your promise of peace is in my heart and mind.

God, I thank You that You love and care for me and are watching over me in every area of my life.

God, I thank You that You are my source and my supply, and no need will go unmet by You.

Philippians 4:4 says, *"Rejoice in the Lord always. Again, I will say, rejoice!"* You can rejoice in God always because you can live confidently understanding that you have a covenant of peace and blessing coming from Him to you, every day of your life, and there is nothing anyone can do to change it. Determine to allow the peace of God to guard your heart, and do so by going to Him in prayer while allowing your petitions and your praises to shape your prayers. It is not complicated. In fact, it is freeing and powerful.

Don't Lose Heart

THE MISSING PEACE

Don't Lose Heart

In the previous chapter, I showed you the importance of guarding your heart and how the peace of God is a weapon He gave you to use in that effort. From the controlling factors of your heart, the issues of your life unfold. Quite often, life can be a roller coaster filled with ups and downs, joyous seasons and sorrowful seasons. Interestingly, there are times when you can be doing better than ever in one area of your life, and simultaneously, worse than ever in another area. I recently read a story about a very successful businessman in El Paso, Texas, where I live. He had reached all new heights in the business and financial community; but, lost one of his children in a tragic car accident. It may not always be that extreme, but there are often contrasts taking place within the different aspects of our lives.

John 16:33 (NIV) says, *"I have told you these things, so that in Me you may have peace. In this world you will have trouble. But take heart! I have overcome the world."* We have looked at this scripture from a different translation in previous chapters, but I want to show you some very important wording here. Jesus is speaking about the reality that in our world, trouble will come. I know that. You know that. We all know that trouble is in the earth. The truth is, you did not need Jesus or a pastor to tell you that you will experience tribulation, tests or trials in one form or another during your life. Every person on this planet has gone through difficult times and seasons and will again in the future. However, Jesus telling us that the reality of trouble existing on the earth is not the important part of this scripture.

Here is what is important:

1. You may have peace
2. Take heart
3. I have overcome the world

Jesus is saying that even during times of trouble, His peace will be in your heart and soul because He has given you the victory over the world. You are a child of God who must walk by faith and not by sight. You are more than a conqueror through Christ Jesus. You are strong in the Lord and in the power of His might. When you are weak, His strength is perfected for your weakness. Greater is He who is in you than he who is in the world. No weapon formed against you shall prosper and any tongue that rises up against you in judgment shall be condemned and proved to be in the wrong. You are the head and not the tail, above and never beneath. God is on your side, and with God on your side, you will have victory over the trouble of the world. It is exactly these promises, along with many others, that empower your heart and mind into a place of peace during times of trouble. You can maintain a tranquil mind in any season, even the worst of them, knowing that health, welfare, prosperity and all sorts of good are coming from God to you. No troubling season can change that promise and reality for you and your family. But please notice, Jesus says, "Take Heart." This phrase is vitally important. So, along with guarding our hearts, we see in certain times, we will need to take heart. The enemy is trying to bring trouble into your life to get you to lose heart. If you can lose something though, that means you can also find it; you can take it back.

The enemy knows he has no power or control over you. The enemy knows if you as a child of God stand in hope and walk by faith, he is defeated in your life. Therefore, the enemy is simply trying to overwhelm you into losing heart. The Bible speaks of fighting the good fight of faith. It is a good fight because it is a fight you are guaranteed to win when you walk by faith. In any fight though, knowing your opponent's plan of attack is always beneficial. Well, Satan's plan of attack in your life is to get you to lose heart. When you lose heart, you quit. When you lose heart, you resign to fate, let go of hope, fall into anxiety and depression. When you lose heart, you live in fear as opposed to faith. That is why Jesus stated over and over throughout the gospels to take heart. **Whatever you do in life, do not lose heart. Do not quit on yourself and do not quit on God.**

November 4, 2008 was a historic day in the United States of America. It is the day that Barack Obama was elected as our 44th President. Whether you voted for him or not, it was a monumental day because he was the first black President to be elected in our country. On that same day, my wife and I flew to Hudson, Florida. We arrived in our hotel room, unpacked for a lengthy stay, and watched as the results of the votes came in. I was nervous. I was scared. I was overwhelmed, and it had nothing to do with who was going to become President of the United States or whether the Republicans or Democrats would control Congress. I was in Florida to undergo back surgery. I was 29 years old and newly married. Life was great, except for the fact I had suffered an intense back injury while working out a few months before that. I was in constant, excruciating pain. There were days I could barely get out of bed. I had violent back spasms almost weekly. One Saturday morning, I had one so bad that I laid in the fetal position in my closet for around thirty minutes by myself, writhing in pain. I managed to crawl like a baby to my bed, but I did not have the strength to actually get into the bed. I had two herniated disks in my lower back. While in Florida, I underwent a minor laser procedure and two herniation repair operations. Karla and I were there for almost two weeks. I felt great. The pain was diminishing, and I knew I was going to be okay. I even remember reminding myself that I was only 29 years old. I was young and would bounce back from this, and that is exactly what I planned on doing.

53

About three years later in 2011, I was still feeling good. I had little to no pain in my back anymore. I was exercising five days a week again and my body was strong. One Saturday, I was at the gym. I had one more exercise to do and I would be done. If you are anything like me, the best part of a workout is finishing the workout. I picked up the relatively light barbell – the one I had been using the entire time, and pain shot through my body. I knew immediately that something was wrong; but somehow, I sensed it was worse this time. I could just tell. It felt different. Sure enough, I had a fully ruptured disk in my lower back. After a couple months, I contacted the same doctor and arranged to go back to Florida to have another operation. This time, I would only need one procedure. I was not nervous. I was not scared. I was not overwhelmed. I knew what to expect and was confident everything was going to be fine. Well, that is not at all how it turned out. The first procedure did not work. I had to have another. After several days, the doctor released me to come home, so I did. I tried to take it easy. After about ten days of being home, I began developing the most severe headaches I had ever experienced in my life. The headaches endured on from a Wednesday through Monday. My wife called the doctor and he explained what an MRI would later confirm: I had what is commonly called a dura leak. I will spare you the graphic description of what a dura leak is. By that Tuesday, the pain in my head began to radiate down my neck and into my lower back where I had the previous surgeries. At one point in the afternoon, I laid down on our couch in so much pain that I realized I literally could not get off the couch. I called my wife. I then called my dad. The next thing I knew I was being airlifted back to Florida for another surgery. As the nurse ran a morphine-filled IV into my veins, I still had hope. I still managed to have faith in the fact that God would heal me, and I was going to be alright eventually. After back surgery number six, I came home for the last time. No offense to anyone from Florida reading this, but other than taking my kids to Disney World, I have no plans to ever go back.

Three months after the last surgery, my back still hurt. I had a radiating pain from my lower back around the right side of my hip that travelled into my stomach and groin. I was worn out physically, mentally, emotionally and spiritually. I was so frustrated. On a Friday morning, my alarm clock went off at 8:23 a.m. When I twisted to reach for my phone to disarm the alarm, I had another back spasm. The pain was excruciating. I could not move. Karla had already left to work for the day, so I was home alone. I do not remember how long I laid there, but it was a while. In that moment, I lost hope. I was defeated. My thoughts turned horribly negative and completely ruled by fear. I remember thinking that I was not even a man anymore. I was never going to be able to exercise again.

Karla was pregnant with our son and I feared that I would not be able to wrestle with him or play catch in the yard. If I ever needed to, how would I even protect my family? As I laid in bed that day, a tear rolled down my face. I can honestly say that I gave up. I was so defeated that I even questioned if I should go on living. I lost heart.

I wonder, is there an area of your life that you have lost heart? Could it be in your marriage, in a relationship with one of your children, in your finances, in your physical well-being, or maybe just in your search for peace? Is there an area, maybe more than one area of your life, that you have given up on or resigned yourself to a belief that it is simply not going to get better? Maybe you have lost heart, but the good news is you can take it back. Hebrews 12:3 (NIV) says, *"Consider Him who endured such opposition from sinners, so that you will not grow weary and lose heart."* The author of the book of Hebrews repeats in verse 5 to not lose heart. To "lose heart" in the literal text means to grow weary, to become discouraged, to lose joy, and to become frustrated. That is exactly what happened to me. Your heart represents your desires, your excitement, and your enthusiasm. Your heart controls the issues of your life; therefore, losing heart will not only determine your failure in that area of your life, but it will also affect every area of your life. When your heart is just not into something, you will not put in the effort to experience the plan God has for you in that area of your life. The scripture I quoted above tells us to consider Jesus who endured so we do not lose heart. You lose heart when you only consider yourself and the situation you are in. You take heart back when you look to Jesus who endured so you too can endure.

55

Here is how you take heart:

■ Listen to the
1 Right Voices

In our incredibly connected lives today, we are inundated with all sorts of voices. People's opinions come into our lives via phone calls, text messages, emails, social media, and personal interactions. Everywhere you turn you find one opinion piece article after another. Quite often, these voices of opinion present themselves as factual, as truth. Yet, they are often just opinion, and not always the truth. With all the information coming at you, it is so easy to listen to the wrong voices of negativity, discouragement, fear and frustration. These voices tend to rob you of your peace, joy and faith. They take you down a path that does not produce health in your heart. All of it is designed to get you to grow weary and lose heart.

A great example of this is found with the nation of Israel when Moses had led them to the promised land God had prepared for them to inhabit and possess, after He freed them from bondage in Egypt. Moses sent twelve men into the land to spy and bring back a report to him and to the people about the cities and inhabitants. As many of you know, ten of the men came back with a negative report and declared they could not inhabit the land. Only two of the men declared the truth — the promise God had given to the nation — and encouraged Moses and all the others to obey God and let Him lead them into the land.

Here is the people's response to Caleb and Joshua's positive report:

Deuteronomy 1:28 — *"Where can we go up? Our brethren have discouraged our hearts, saying, 'The people are greater and taller than we; the cities are great and fortified up to heaven; moreover we have seen the sons of the Anakim there.'"*

Ten men discouraged the hearts of over three million people and caused them to completely miss out on their destiny and the fulfillment of God's promise for their lives, their families and their nation. How? Because they listened to the wrong voices and rejected the right ones. They rejected the voice of God and they rejected the voice of two Godly men. The Bible says that the truth will set you free. **To take heart, the priority of your life must be to find truth, not opinion.** The world and Satan will always try to contradict God's truth for your life. The enemy will try to make your problems and challenges seem insurmountable. He will use people's negativity and doubt to get you to lose heart and quit. The nation of Israel did not possess the promised land for another forty years until their children, led by Joshua and Caleb, came back and overcame the challenges within the land. They stood on God's truth and His promise.

Please understand that God's promise is going to be fulfilled. The nation of Israel would possess the promised land because God said they would. So, the question is not if God will do what He said; the question is, will you? The enemy wants you to miss out on God's promise, just like the nation of Israel, by intimidating you into losing heart and not pursuing what God told you would be yours. Will you be like the ten spies and live outside of your destiny, or will you be like Joshua and Caleb and trust that God is faithful? Take heart today knowing that He is greater than any challenge or obstacle in your life. Do not worry about what society says, what your friends say or what the cynics say. Focus on what God says about your situation. Remember, Jesus gave you His Word so in Him you will have peace. In the world, you will have trouble, but take heart, He has overcome the world.

■ Remember Your Source
2 of Peace and Victory

There is no way I would ever be able to fully comprehend what you have gone through or are going through in your life. Some of you have faced incredible circumstance. It is safe to assume there are people reading this book who have gone through painful divorces, were molested or abused, have committed crimes and faced severe consequences, and many other incredibly challenging situations. It would be completely disingenuous of me to even pretend I can comprehend the pain and hurt many of you have had to deal with. But I will tell you this: there is still victory and healing for you. The good news is that I do not need to understand because God does. I am not your answer; He is! Regardless of your past or present challenges, God has the solution. He is your greatest resource to get through the obstacle that is in your path right now. The danger is to get overwhelmed by the circumstance or the size of the challenge in your life. The moment you look at the size of the challenge and not the strength of your Savior Jesus, you will lose heart.

Let's go back to the nation of Israel in another instance. They were at war with the Philistine army and being openly mocked and tormented by a giant man named Goliath. The army of Israel was terrified. A young man named David, who would eventually become King of Israel, came into the camp to bring food to his brothers who were fighting with the Israelites. David was a shepherd boy. He was not a warrior, and yet he volunteered to confront Goliath. Read what he says to King Saul before going to face the giant.

1 SAMUEL 17:32

"Let no man's heart fail because of him."

The truth is the men had already lost heart. They were terrified and not even wanting to enter the fight anymore. They had completely forgotten God was for them; but, not David. His advice still rings true today: do not lose heart because there is a giant in your life. Take heart knowing God has armed you for battle and prepared victory to come into your life. Do not lose heart for the battle. Do not lose heart for your dreams. Do not lose heart to pursue and realize the fulfillment of God's promises in your life. Facing a giant is not fun. It is not always easy. It is never the plan or the desire, but you must face it anyway. Please understand that the purpose of the giant in your life is to get your heart to fail, to cause you to lose heart and not fight for what you want. Take heart knowing God is on your side and He will give you the victory.

■ Walk by Faith,
3 Not by Sight

In 2008, a man in our church approached me after a Sunday morning service to inform me that he and his wife were not going to be able to give their offering anymore. You may recall that America was in the midst of a housing crisis that drove the national economy into a deep and painful recession. It was the worst recession the United States had endured since the Great Depression in the early 1900s. Millions of businesses closed. Unemployment skyrocketed. People lost their jobs, their cars and their houses. It was a dark time in our country. When he told me this news, I immediately felt empathy for him and his family, as I assumed they had been financially affected by what was going on. As it turned out, they had not. He and his wife both still had their jobs with no danger of losing them. He said to me, "In this economy, who can still give to charities and churches?" I remember thinking, "Well, *you* can." Of course, I was far more diplomatic than that and just tried to encourage and reassure him.

Like this man, we often allow the issues of society to become our issues even though society's issues are not directly affecting us. This poses a real obstacle in the pursuit of peace. We get spooked by what is happening in politics, in the news or just in society in general. I have met so many people over the years who carry far too much unnecessary anxiety, fear and stress. You have enough to deal with in life. You do not need to be weighed down by added pressure that actually has no effect on your everyday life. This is truly a great lesson to learn. Do not be bogged down by unnecessary worry. Do not be burdened by things you cannot control. The truth is, worrying about them will not change them in the least. You take care of what you can control. What you can control is what is allowed to rule your heart. Guard your heart. Take heart.

As Christians, we are told to walk by faith and not by sight. You cannot be ruled by what you see. You must be ruled by God's Word and His provision for your life. Of course, that does not mean you ignore what is going on around you. A life of faith is not a reckless or foolish life. It is not ignorance or pretending like a problem is not real. A life of faith is a life of pursuing truth and wisdom while trusting God to lead you in and through any situation you are in. **A life of faith is one that says your God-given promise is greater than your world-produced problem.** A life of faith is one determined to never give up and never quit in the face of resistance.

Jeremiah 51:46 — *"And lest your heart faint, and you fear for the rumor that will be heard in the land (a rumor will come one year, and after that, in another year a rumor will come, and violence in the land, ruler against ruler)."*

When you believe the rumors in the land, you will lose heart. As you know, there is always something going on. If you look hard enough, you will find doom and gloom, conspiracy theories, negativity and fear. Our current news and political environment thrive on this type of rhetoric, and it is not going to change. In fact, every generation that has lived has dealt with incredible challenges and obstacles. There is always something, but there is also always God. Rumors in the land do not remove His promise of peace for your life. Verse 48 of that same chapter in Jeremiah says, *"But God will deliver you."* Take heart today and remember that Jesus is your Savior. Too often, we only view Jesus as our Savior for eternity, but He is our Savior every day of our lives. No matter what is going on in the land, Jesus is your Savior, Deliverer and Redeemer. You can put your eyes on the doom and gloom of the world and lose heart, be tormented by anxiety and riddled with fear; or, you can look to Him and walk by faith. Remember, He is the author and finisher of your faith. Do not lose heart. Do not lose your faith because times get tough. Faith is the overcoming power of God that allows you to endure tough times and come through them stronger, wiser and more creative in spite of their challenges.

After all I had been through during the 4th, 5th and 6th back surgeries, at the beginning of 2012, I found myself in what I now understand to be a minor depression. Like I mentioned, I was still in constant pain and I felt so defeated. Our son Caleb was born that June, a month after my mother was diagnosed with Stage 4 ovarian cancer. Such sadness abounded at the news of my mother's diagnosis, followed by such great joy at the arrival of our first-born child. That year ended with my mom passing away two days after my sister had her first-born daughter. I was not okay mentally, emotionally, spiritually or physically, but I remember knowing I could not allow myself to stay that way. I had a wife to love, a church to pastor, a child to raise, and a God-given promise of a peace-filled life to live. I had to take heart, and that is exactly what I did. If I could do it, so can you. It's okay if you have lost heart, but now go take it back. I am not depressed anymore. My body is stronger than it has ever been. My wife and I have a wonderful marriage with two beautiful children. Our church is reaching more people for God's glory than it ever has before. We walk by faith. We take heart.

A Fresh Start

THE MISSING PEACE

A Fresh Start

Have you ever felt like life was out of control? Have you ever found yourself in a circumstance filled with disappointment or frustration and asked, "How did I get here?" Have you ever felt like you just could not catch a break because things simply were not working out for you?

We live in such a unique world. Within it are billions of people with varying backgrounds, passions, dreams, desires and personal agendas. No two people are alike, and none of us are perfect. That is part of the beauty and the complication of the world we live in. We all make mistakes. We make good and bad choices. We are foolish sometimes. We behave badly and say things that are hurtful. We have good days and bad days and at some point, we all find ourselves in the middle of somewhat chaotic situations we did not expect. The question is, where did the chaos come from? While some chaos is out of your control, the base truth is **the quality of your life will be determined by the quality of your choices.** There is no getting around this reality. If you make good choices, the consequences of those choices will be good and vice versa.

Chaos is defined as a state of utter confusion and disorder. Chaos results in increased stress, anxiety, panic and worry. Sometimes, even worse. Everyone deals with confusion and disorder. Other than completely removing yourself from society by going off the grid somewhere in the middle of nowhere, there is just no perfect way to completely avoid chaotic circumstances. No matter how hard you try, your choices will never be perfect. Additionally, your

63

life is deeply connected to other people who make imperfect choices which can spill chaos into your life.

Let me tell you, the most important thing to deal with in these types of situations is yourself. You cannot always control what happens to you or around you, but you can control what happens inside of you. John Mroz, the founder and CEO of the East West Institute, best known for its involvement in diplomatic and foreign affairs in the Middle East, made this incredible statement: "Peace is not the absence of chaos or conflict, but rather finding yourself in the midst of that chaos and remaining calm in your heart." Life is not always orderly. Even the best plans do not always result in the intended consequence, but you can maintain peace even when chaos arises. Your joy and happiness do not have to be ruled by outside forces. God shows you in the Bible His ability to help you in these circumstances. He also shows you what role you play in it.

As 2019 ended and 2020 began, expectation filled our lives. The United States was experiencing economic prosperity at levels we had not experienced in years. Companies were growing and expanding. Wages were increasing. People were travelling and going on amazing vacations. Our church had incredible plans. We were finalizing remodeling plans for our third church campus in downtown El Paso. Excitement abounded all around, but it would not stay that way. By March, everything changed. It really is incredible how quickly life can get flipped upside down. As the COVID-19 pandemic broke out around the world, our normal lives were completely disrupted. At the time I wrote this book in the first quarter of 2021, tens of millions of people had been infected by the Coronavirus. Families were separated by travel restrictions and social distancing laws. Hundreds of thousands of people had died and lives were shattered. There was economic devastation. Countless businesses were forced to close, many permanently. Millions of jobs were lost. By April of 2020, nations around the world issued stay-at-home orders, and anxiety increased over 39%. Our sense of normalcy in early 2020 had been lost. I, along with the incredible pastoral team at our church, took over 1,500 prayer calls and 300 counseling appointments during a five-month span. So many people I spoke to and prayed with expressed in some way, shape or form that their life felt out of control. As I spoke to people, I quickly began to recognize a pattern. The pandemic is what initiated the problems, but choices and behaviors exhibited during it is what exasperated those problems into chaos.

Like we experienced in 2020, sometimes situations beyond our control dramatically affect our plans, our dreams and our lives, but that is usually not the case. You and I are typically in control of our lives. In fact, no one can actually control you. Not God. Not Satan. Not your spouse. Not your employer. Not your supervisor. Not your friends. Not the government. You cannot control every situation you are in. You cannot control the people around you. You cannot control how your friends and family react to societal issues, but you can control yourself. Therefore, how you respond to the events of life becomes vitally important to your overall peace and happiness, particularly if you are responding to your own mistakes or failures. The most important thought you can keep in your mind to help you take heart in these types of situations is that God is with you, and so too is His peace. Jesus said in John 14:27, *"Peace I leave with you, My peace I give to you; not as the world gives do I give to you. Let not your heart be troubled, neither let it be afraid."* Why do we tend to believe God is only with us in the good times? Why do we tend to immediately resort to fear? God is with you in the worst of times. He is with you even when you have failed. He is with you when you have sinned and are paying the consequence of that sin. And in those moments, His peace is still being delivered onto your life. That is truly the evidence of the mercy of God.

We see a great example of this in Psalm 51 as King David calls out to God for forgiveness in the aftermath of his affair with Bathsheba. What began as an affair turned into conspiracy to commit murder, murder and cover-up. It also produced years of turmoil within David's family. One of his children dies, another rapes his sister, and another even leads an insurrection against his father in an attempt to overthrow him as king. In Psalm 51, David has been visited by Nathan, the great prophet of God in the nation of Israel. The King is grieved. He is overwhelmed by the negative fallout caused by his terrible and sinful decision making. This is not the first time nor the last time we see King David calling out to God in the midst of trouble. As foolish as David was at times, and as serious as the consequences he faced due to his foolishness were, he was always wise enough to turn back to God.

Psalm 51:1-12 — *"Have mercy upon me, O God, according to Your lovingkindness; according to the multitude of Your tender mercies, blot out my transgressions. Wash me thoroughly from my iniquity, and cleanse me from my sin. For I acknowledge my transgressions, and my sin is always before me. Against You, You only, have I sinned, and done this evil in Your sight— that You may be found just when You speak, and blameless when You judge. Behold, I was brought forth in iniquity, and in sin my mother conceived me. Behold, You desire truth in the inward parts, and in the hidden part You will make me to know wisdom. Purge me with hyssop, and I shall be clean; wash me, and I shall be whiter than snow. Make me hear joy and gladness, that the bones You have broken may rejoice. Hide Your face from my sins, and blot out all my iniquities. Create in me a clean heart, O God, and renew a steadfast spirit within me. Do not cast me away from Your presence, and do not take Your Holy Spirit from me. Restore to me the joy of Your salvation, and uphold me by Your generous Spirit."*

66

In verse 1, he immediately asks God to give him mercy. David, minus having a personal relationship with Jesus, lived a grace-filled life. He understood the grace and mercy of God like few ever had. There is a great lesson to be learned here. Like David, you live under the undeserved and unearned favor of God. The enemy will always attempt to separate you from God through the guilt or shame of your transgression. You cannot let him accomplish what he is trying to do. You cannot let him win that battle within your soul. Romans 5 teaches us that God's response to sin is to give us grace. God hates sin, but more importantly, He also forgives it. How incredible to know that where sin abounds, God's grace abounds much more! David always ran to God. He ran to God in the best of times. He ran to God in the worst of times. He ran to God in his victories. He ran to God in his defeats. No matter what, David ran to God and God always responded with His tender loving kindness. Like David, you must run to God in every circumstance, particularly when life is filled with turmoil.

Psalms 51:10 — *"Create in me a clean heart, O God, and renew a steadfast spirit within me."*

What an interesting prayer to pray. David cries out to God for Him to "create in me a clean heart". We must note that David is calling upon the creative power of God. This power belongs to God and God only. The creative power of God has nothing to do with your abilities or talents, and somehow David knew to ask God for it in that moment. Remember, this is one of the worst moments of his life, and he is asking for a clean heart. Logic, or human nature, would not think this way. We would think David needs to pay for what he has done. His actions were abhorrent. Cancel culture would come after him. Thank God, Jesus is not in the canceling business. Clearly, David recognized the need to guard his heart and to take heart, but he knew he could not do it alone. Just as David called upon the creative power of God, so can you. Remember, this is the greatest power in the universe. This is the force that powers the peace of God beyond your understanding. This is the power that created the heavens and the earth, the land and the seas, the sun and the moon. The creative power of God is what spoke man into existence. God speaks through His creative power, and what He speaks, happens.

PSALMS 51:10 (MESSAGE)

"God, make a fresh start in me, shape a Genesis week from the chaos of my life."

The Message translation reveals that the creative power of God produces a "Genesis week" in our lives, even during chaotic times. A Genesis week is a season of new beginnings. It is a fresh start! God is the God of new beginnings. He does not care about your past. He only cares about your present to get you to the wonderful future He has planned for you. His creative power can usurp the chaos of your life and bring peace and restore purpose. David sinned greatly. He got away from his calling and purpose as King of Israel. He made horrible decisions that bore terrible results in his and others' lives, yet God responded to his prayer and gave him a fresh start. God is so grand, and His character is so vast, that He is beyond comprehension or simple explanation. He does not fit in a little box. He cannot be described with one name or a couple adjectives. I say this because the "Genesis week" not only highlights God's creative power, but it also reminds us that He is the Alpha and Omega, the beginning and the end. Please know that in every ending, like David experienced, God has a new beginning. He is never finished with you. Romans 11:29 says, *"For the gifts and the calling of God are irrevocable."* Nothing you do will change the fact that God has a genesis week designed for you. Be encouraged today! Your new beginning is here! New joy! New hope! New wisdom! New favor! New opportunities! New relationships! New healing! New success! New intentions! New creativity! New faith! New victory! New ideas! New solutions! New restoration! New outcomes! New freedom! New peace! God is the God of new things and He is going to work new things in your life! God does not need a new year to give you a new beginning. God does not need everything in your life to be perfect to give you a fresh start. He has not left you. He has not forgotten you. A failed business, a divorce, a global pandemic or any other situation cannot override God's plans for your future. He is the God of order. He does not care anymore what you have done. He is with you to give you a clean slate, a Genesis week! Do you believe it? If you don't, it is time to start.

Every great promise of God set out before you comes with the opportunity for you to respond to it. Everything God says, He does. Everything God touches, He blesses. He wants you to live free from chaos, knowing you can take heart and overcome trouble, realizing a life of peace and happiness. The question is, are you going to live a life in line with what He wants to do for you, or are you going to let your decisions and actions contradict His work in your life? Yes, God will always respond to you when you call upon Him in times of trouble, but life is much easier when we simply avoid creating those situations altogether. King David could have avoided the entire mess he was in by not having an affair with Bathsheba. Had he gone to war like he was supposed to, had he not broken his own law and gone up to the roof at night to watch her bathe, or had he just not slept with her, he would have never been in this situation in the first place.

Throughout the first chapter of Genesis, as God created the universe as we know it, we see the phrase "yields according to its own kind." You must recognize in life that everything produces after its own kind. This is one of the laws of the universe that God spoke into existence. Just like the law of gravity, this law is indiscriminate of people, place or time. It works, good or bad, for everyone in exactly the same way. Everything produces after its own kind. Love produces love. Hate produces hate. Love does not produce hate. Dogs produce dogs. Cats produce cats. Dogs do not produce cats. Apple seeds produce apple trees. Orange seeds produce orange trees. Apple seeds do not produce orange trees. Good decisions produce good consequences. If you are kind to your spouse, kindness will be plentiful in your marriage. If you live within your means, you will be able to save money and have financial stability. If you do not, you will be in debt. Too often, people want the results of good decisions without exhibiting good behavior. That is just not how life works.

1 Corinthians 14:40 says, *"Let all things be done decently and in order."* God is the God of order and not chaos; so, whatever is chaotic in your life is not Godly. You cannot exist in chaos and claim Godliness. God does not produce chaos, therefore, neither should you. God tells you in His Word that He has set before you blessing and cursing, life and death. In Deuteronomy, He implores you to choose life! You have options in your life, and you choose which option you will pick. You can go to church or not go. You can eat healthy food or not. You can lose your temper with your spouse or not. You can work hard on your job or not. You can be diligent or not. Everyone one of those choices and thousands of others will produce a result. Don't make terrible decisions and then be mad at God or the people around you because you do not like the consequences your decisions produced in your life. So, I pose this question to you now: are the decisions you are currently making in life ones that will produce peace? Not always, but often, we are missing the peace we so deeply desire simply because we are not making decisions that will produce our desired results.

"Blessed are the peacemakers," Jesus said in Matthew 5:9. You can, and should, be a peacemaker. That word "blessed" means to be enviably happy. Happiness is a product of peace. More importantly, it is the result of making peace. Remember, one of the definitions of peace is health, welfare, prosperity and every kind of good. Now

69

is the time to start making healthy decisions for your marriage, your body, your career and every other area of your life. Those healthy decisions will produce welfare and prosperity, consequently opening the door for happiness to be far more present in your life. The Apostle Paul wrote in Romans that peace comes to those who do good! It is amazing how much peace inhabits your soul when you live to do good. You know the difference between good and bad, it is just a matter of whether or not you will choose good. You are called by God to break the cycle of disruption, retaliation and chaos so many people live in. There will always be opposition in your life. There will always be things or people who come against you. Along the path of life, you will encounter others who are just not good people. You do not have to stoop down to their level. An eye for an eye only results in two people who cannot see. You can change the pattern of dissention, strife and unforgiveness in your life by choosing to be a peacemaker. The more you choose that path, the more peace enters your life and the lives of the people around you. Then, you have less to worry about. You have less negative fallout from bad choices. You have less stressful interactions with coworkers, your boss and your acquaintances. You do good, you get good. Everything produces after its own kind. You make peace, you enjoy peace!

King David was a man of passion, vision and dreams. He had a dream to build God an incredible temple so the nation of Israel could worship and glorify their Heavenly Father. After all the pain of his decisions, he could have easily given up on that great dream, but he did not. Ultimately, his son Solomon would build the temple, but David laid out all the provision for it to be built. At the moment David made the decision to have an affair, his life was full of promise and potential. Because he ran to God after his mistake, the potential of his future was not erased. He went on to become one of the greatest men to ever live. He is highly regarded and revered by millions of people and has been for generations. Regardless of where your life is today, your future is full of promise and potential. Is there a dream in your heart that you have given up on because of bad decisions? Is there a vision you had for your future that you now feel is lost because of the consequence of your choices? God has not given up on you, and neither should you! He is the dream giver and the dream fulfiller! I dare you to dream once again. I challenge you to ask God to restore a fresh vision for your life. He gave you those dreams knowing the mistakes you were going to make along the way. He has not lost interest in you or your plans. It is time for a fresh start filled with new beginnings. Go choose life over death, blessing over cursing, order over chaos and peace over trouble. Like David, your Genesis week is upon you, now go chase the amazing future God has in store for you.

Take A Stand

Take A Stand

In the United States of America, we are very accustomed to discussing, enjoying and declaring our freedoms. We live in the land of the free and the home of the brave. We are a free people with the right to speak, vote, worship and do as we please within the laws of our land. These freedoms are afforded to the citizens of the U.S.A. by the United States Constitution and the Bill of Rights. Our country is by no means perfect, but I do hope we have not, and will never, take for granted the opportunities and freedoms we have simply because we are in the United States. Of course, when you talk about freedom within countries, you are talking about man-made freedoms. These freedoms allow governance to be placed within a community to define the way the people live within that society. As you know, man-made freedom is not completely literal. As free as the United States is, there are still laws that govern our cities, our states and our nation. If you choose to break those laws, depending on the severity of the action, your freedom can be taken away from you. These freedoms I speak of are incredible. They are amazing. They allow us to dream and achieve as a people and as a nation. Millions of men and women have paid the ultimate price to defend these liberties, but as great as they are, they are not the ultimate freedom.

The greatest freedom is God-given. This is the freedom that truly matters; it transforms your life into a life of peace and happiness. You can exist in a free society, but can still feel like you are living in a prison. Too many people are prisoners to regret, shame, guilt and disappointment. Sure, they are free to come and go as they

"Therefore if the Son makes you free, you shall be free indeed."

please. They are free to vote for whomever they feel will serve as the best senator or president. They are free to go to whatever type of church they so desire, but they are not truly free within their soul. This bondage robs them of the life of peace God wants them to possess and enjoy, but there is an answer. John 8:36 says, *"Therefore if the Son makes you free, you shall be free indeed."* As Jesus spoke these words of freedom to His disciples and the Jewish followers who surrounded Him, the nation of Israel was not a free people. They were literally living in captivity to the Roman Empire. Yet, He spoke of freedom anyway. The freedom Jesus gives you exists internally and manifests externally. His freedom is divine, it is supernatural, and it is eternal in nature. Mostly, it is very personal and given to you so you can maximize your life. If you are a Christian, you are free. Jesus died on the cross for your freedom. He paid the ultimate price with His life, so you do not have to. Because of the sacrifice Jesus made, any person who believes in Him has the opportunity move their lives forward with a passion to chase their dreams, find fulfillment and success, and build a wonderful life without living in bondage to their past failures and mistakes. The best days of your life, mentally and emotionally, are ahead of you thanks to this incredible gift. Freedom is in your hands; go live free!

Galatians 5:1 (Message) — *"Christ has set us free to live a free life. So take your stand! Never again let anyone put a harness of slavery on you."*

Take a Stand!

Christ has set you free! Free from the curse of sin and death. Free from the power of the enemy. Free to overcome the world. Free

74

from the shame of your past. Free from any bondage in relation to lack, torment or condemnation. You are free! You did not earn this freedom, but the grace of God has delivered it to you anyway. This is truly one of the greatest gifts any person can receive. It is also the most important reality for you to allow into your life of peace as you guard your heart. So why do so many Christians not live free? Why is it that millions of believers live bound to panic, depression, regret or guilt? Why is it that peace is missing? The above scripture in Galatians 5 is incredibly revealing beyond the fact that Jesus set you free: "So, take your stand." There it is! That is as important a statement as the statement on freedom itself. As you guard your heart and as you take heart in times of challenge, you must internally decide that no matter what goes on in your life, you will take a stand for what God has done and is doing for you. God has given you freedom, but scripture clearly reveals you will have to fight to maintain it. Freedom is received, but it can also be lost. Fighting for freedom is not a foreign concept though. Millions have fought and even died for freedom for thousands of years. Christianity has been fighting this fight since Jesus died on the cross. Let me also say, this is not something to worry about. The Bible says we fight the good fight of faith. Well, the only good fight is the fight you are going to win, and faith gives us the victory to overcome the world.

The Word of God very clearly states numerous times that we as Christians are in the world, but we are not supposed to be of the world. Why is that? The answer is simple really: the world system is a lie. God's system is truth, and the truth exists to set you free from the ramifications of lies. Everything about the world system is designed and created to put you into some form of bondage. The world promises joy, freedom and satisfaction, but only delivers misery, oppression and emptiness. As I went through my late teens and early twenties, I did not serve God. I was a typical high school and college-age person who was solely interested in living the party life. I was the cliché pastor's kid, or PK, that went wild. I smoked. I drank a lot, at times uncontrollably. I had tons of friends. You know, I was having fun. Yet, in all that fun, I was completely miserable. I was told that this fun was supposed to produce happiness, but I was anxious, addicted, lonely and far from God. To compound the misery, for about five years, I battled severe insomnia. It was awful. In fact, it was by far the worst years of my life. I searched for peace and happiness in the world only to discover a black hole of darkness. I did not find peace until I turned my life back to God's Word and started living in His ways. True peace is only realized with Jesus. I had to take a stand, and that included looking in the mirror and deciding to put my life on a different path. Yes, I turned to the Lord, but I also had to make better choices, stop behaving the same way I had been, and even surround myself with different people. When I did, Jesus began to set me free. He gave me peace. He delivered me from darkness to light. God does not play favorites. His promise of freedom is not limited to a select few. He is no respecter of persons, so if He delivered me, He will do it for you; but, you must also take a stand against the ways of the world. There is only one true freedom, and it is found in Jesus Christ.

Romans 8:1-2 (Message) — *"With the arrival of Jesus, the Messiah, that fateful dilemma is resolved. Those who enter into Christ's being here for us no longer have to live under a continuous, low lying black cloud. A new power is in operation! The Spirit of life in Christ, like a strong wind, has magnificently cleared the air, freeing you from a fated life of brutal tyranny at the hands of sin and death."*

God is so good. He sent Jesus to change the course of history for mankind and all those who would believe in Him. He took the power of sin away from the enemy and gave the power of victory to all those who believe in Him. Be encouraged by the reality that Satan has no power over you. He cannot control you. He cannot rule you. He cannot overcome you. The Word says to resist the devil and he will flee from you. You do not have to fight the devil. Jesus already fought that fight and won it decisively. You do not have to overcome the devil. Jesus already overcame him. You do not have to overpower the enemy. Jesus already took the power away from him and gave it to you. What do you have to do? Take a stand! That is it. Take a stand and he will flee from you. You are a child of God and you are more than a conqueror through Jesus Christ. God has removed the dark cloud of condemnation over your life. You no longer are bound to your mistakes, failures or regrets. You are free to live a peaceful life with a future full of hope. Jesus has declared you free.

In the previous chapters, you learned the importance of guarding your heart, for out of it flows the issues and boundaries of your life. The Bible also says that out of the abundance of the heart, the mouth speaks. If God declared you free, it is time for you to start declaring your freedom as well. As a Christian, God has given you the right to proclaim what is yours in Christ Jesus. A couple years ago, I created a list of confessions that I declare over myself almost daily. I call them, **My Freedom Declared**, and I am going to share them with you. I want you to write these down, put them in the notes on your phone, or take a picture of them. Start confessing them every day of your life to encourage yourself, to take heart and to build your faith.

I am free from the curse of sin and death! I am a child of God!

I am free from the power of the enemy! I am an overcomer!

I am free from my past mistakes, failures and guilt! I am forgiven!

I am free from brokenness and destruction! I am restored and recovered!

I am free from bondage, anxiety and depression! I have the peace of God!

I am free from fear and torment! I walk by faith and not by sight!

I am free from sickness and disease! I am healed!

I am free from overburden and discouragement! I take heart in Jesus!

I am free from deception! I live in truth and the truth sets me free!

I am free from self-doubt and insecurity! I am a believer and God is with me!

Living Free!

President Franklin D. Roosevelt is quoted as saying, "In the truest sense, freedom cannot be bestowed; it must be achieved." This statement is completely accurate from a social perspective regarding human and societal freedom; however, God is not bound to humanity. He has in fact bestowed freedom upon all who believe in Him. With that said, I think what the great President said still bears some relevance in our daily lives. You now know that you are free. You are now aware you can believe in your freedom and even declare it over your life; but, we all know that words minus action mean very little. "Take a stand," the scripture says, and "Never again let anyone put a harness of slavery on you." You do play a part in your freedom. The world will always try to rob you of the free life God has blessed you with. You must decide to not just believe and not just speak, but to live free.

▰ Free to Think Big,
1 Believe Big and Live Big

Let me tell you something: you are amazing! Did you know that? Most people do not believe that about themselves. Too often, our insecurities, our mistakes and our failures weigh us down mentally and emotionally to the point that we accept a lesser view of ourselves. The lie of anxiety and depression makes you begin to think your life is stuck where it is. You believe you will only accomplish so much, and you are bound to the problems and burdens you are currently experiencing. The result of this thinking is a mediocre, small life. How is it possible for me to tell you that you are amazing without knowing you? Easy. God is amazing. You are created in His image; therefore, you are amazing as well.

2 Corinthians 6:11–13 (Message) — *"Dear, dear Corinthians, I can't tell you how much I long for you to enter this wide–open, spacious life. We didn't fence you in. The smallness you feel comes from within you. Your lives aren't small, but you're living them in a small way. I'm speaking as plainly as I can and with great affection. Open up your lives. Live openly and expansively!"*

This is one of my favorite scriptures in the Bible. It encourages me, and I hope it will also encourage you. It is encouraging because it shows you the lifestyle God wants you to pursue. He wants you to live a wide–open, spacious life. God does not desire for you to live a small, fenced in life ruled my mediocrity and disappointment. He is the God of wonder and He has an amazing future planned for you. A future where He is working for you to empower you into success, joy, fulfilled dreams and a peace-filled life. Now is your time to remove the fence and expand your thinking to build an amazing life. No more should you allow small-mindedness, lack, defeat or a poverty mentality to stop you from achieving great things. From this moment forward, you are not going to be held back anymore. You are going to open up your life and live expansively just like God wants you to. The Bible says all God's promises are YES and AMEN for you. When I read that scripture years ago, I decided I am going to accept nothing less than the fulfillment of every great work God has in store for me and my family. If God said you can have it, then decide you are going to have it. If God said you can do something, then decide you are going to do it. If God said you can be it, then decide you are going to be it. Don't let your past stop you. Don't let your mistakes stop you. Don't let your insecurities stop you. Don't let the people around you stop you. They are just trying to fence you in. There is a wide-open, spacious life waiting for you to possess and enjoy. You serve a big God with big plans for you. Your life does not have to be lived in a small way. Open up your life to big thinking and big believing. It is time to start dreaming and pursuing a great vision for your future, filled with God's peace and blessing raining down on your life.

2 Free to Press On

Jesus drew a very clear line in the sand in the book of John when He told us that the thief comes only to steal, to kill and to destroy; but, He came to give us life and life more abundantly. Too often, people simply do not enjoy the abundant life Jesus wants them to have because they are stuck in the past. Let me tell you, God is the God of right now. He cares about your present because He wants you to have a wonderful future. He does not and never will care about your past. One of the easiest ways the enemy separates us from peace, hope and faith for a great future is to get us to live bound to the past. This is one of the unhealthiest ways to live. In fact, it is toxic and completely destructive within your heart and mind. The mistakes, failures and sins of your past need to stay where they belong — behind you. If you focus on the past, what is behind you will only keep you behind. The simplest example I can give you is driving. Picture yourself in your vehicle in the fast lane on the highway. Where do your eyes need to be the vast majority of the time to avoid a crash? The answer is obvious. Your eyes need to be on the road ahead. If you constantly look in the rear-view mirror, you will not see what it is taking place in front of you, and you will either miss your exit or hit another vehicle. Either way, the result is you do not get where you intended to go. The same is true in life. You cannot live chained to your past. Living your life focused on the past will only produce a life of missed opportunities, stagnation and frustration. You will not get to the life God wants you to enjoy.

Philippians 3:13-14 — *"Brethren, I do not count myself to have apprehended; but one thing I do, forgetting those things which are behind and reaching forward to those things which are ahead, I press toward the goal for the prize of the upward call of God in Christ Jesus."*

My beautiful 4-year-old daughter Charlotte loves the Disney movie *Frozen*. If we have watched it once in our house, we have watched it one hundred times. She knows every line of every scene spoken by every character in the movie. If you have a young daughter like me, the chances are pretty good you have seen Frozen many times as well. In the movie, the main character named Elsa sings a world-famous song called "Let It Go." The main lyric says, "Let it go, let it go, can't hold it back anymore." A couple thousand years after the great Apostle Paul wrote the book of Philippians and told us the one thing to do is to forget the past, we are still having to remind ourselves to do this very thing. Notice that Paul then says to press toward the goal. You only have to press on something if there is resistance. Of course, there is resistance though. The enemy does not want you to press on. He wants you to quit, to give up on yourself, and to live in misery. He does not want you to enjoy the wide-open, spacious life Jesus came to give you. Yes, you will have resistance in pursuing your dreams and letting go of your past, but you must press on anyway. Here is how I look at this: I resist resistance. When the enemy wants a fight, I fight back. When the enemy brings up my past, I remind myself of what God says about my future. When life knocks me down, I get back up. I am not going to be robbed of the life God has for me, and neither should you. It is time to take a stand and reach toward the call of God on your life, the calling of peace.

God has too great a future planned for you for Satan to just wave the white flag of surrender without trying to stop you from realizing God's plans. He is at least going to make an attempt to keep you bound to your past and stop you from moving forward. He knows you will not doubt yourself if you do not consider the shortcomings of your past. You will not have unforgiveness weighing you down if you do not consider the hurt of your past. You will not have trust issues if you do not consider the betrayal of your past. You will not be jealous or envious if you do not consider the past. You will not hate someone if you do not consider the issues of your past. You will not fear the future if you do not consider the failure of your past. You have been set free; it is time to live free.

My next statement is incredibly blunt, but because I want the best for you, I am going to speak the truth. It is time to let the past be in the past. Like the song says, "let it go!" I know it is hard. I know the pain is deep. How long are you going to let the banner of disappointment hang over your life? It is time to press on. It is time to move forward. Your past is not who you are. You do not have to allow it to define you anymore. You are a new creation in Christ Jesus. He loves you and He forgives you. It is time for you to forgive yourself as well, and be free from your past. Every mistake comes with some form of a negative consequence. We have all dealt with them, and will in the future, but you should not allow those mistakes to cause unnecessary and additional damage by carrying the past into your present decision making, thinking and behavior. Do not give your past more power than it deserves. Do not give your past authority over your future.

Isaiah 43:18-19 — *"Do not remember the former things, nor consider the things of old. Behold, I will do a new thing, now it shall spring forth; shall you not know it? I will even make a road in the wilderness and rivers in the desert."*

Once again, we see the importance of not letting the past destroy our future. God is the God of new things. Too many people miss

"I will bless you and you shall be a blessing."

out on the new opportunities God has for them simply because their focus is not on the present, but on the past. It is not that the opportunity did not come, it is that they missed it because they were not looking for it; they were not prepared for it. The above scripture really highlights the magnificence of God's plan for you. Not only does He not remember the former thing and promise to do a new thing for you, He shows us that nothing can stop His work in your life. Notice the imagery in the above scripture of a wilderness and a desert. Both can be extremely dangerous if you are in them lost and without resource. Both the wilderness and the desert represent what the enemy wants to do with your past. He wants you to be lost without direction or abandoned without hope, but remember, God is your source and your supply. He is the God who provides. God knows you will find yourself in a wilderness at times, yet He will provide a road through it. He knows at times you may be in a dry land, yet He will create rivers through the desert. Rivers of provision, health, prosperity, tranquility, forgiveness and freedom. All you need to do is press on and stop considering the things of old. God wants to do a new thing, so let it spring forth in your life.

82

▬ Free to Be a Force
3 for Good

Everything God does for you as His child is done for several reasons. He absolutely gave you freedom for your benefit, but He also gave it to you for His glory and for the benefit of others. God's blessing and provision in your life is meant to make your life better while also improving the lives of people around you. Genesis 12:2 says, *"I will bless you and you shall be a blessing."* The purpose behind God's blessing will always include you being a blessing. You are not supposed to be a swamp of God's favor and peace, but rather a river. The goodness of God is meant to flow through you, not just in you. Truly, this is an amazing opportunity we all have in life. Every person on this great planet of ours can make a difference. Jesus told us it is truly more blessed to give than to receive. I agree with that statement with all my heart, but I did not fully understand it until I had children of my own. I always loved birthdays and Christmas. Who doesn't, right? But I never loved them like I do now. The joy of seeing my children open their presents is like nothing I have ever experienced before. During the global COVID-19 pandemic of 2020, our church partnered with a local food bank and we gave over 100,000 boxes of food and supplies to people in need during that intense season. We donated over 50,000 masks to our community. We gave 1,500 backpacks full of school supplies to children whose families were facing financial hardship. The week before Christmas, we gave 4,000 families a full Christmas meal and handed out 8,000 toys to young children in our community. These are life-changing events our church participates in. I will never forget the moment a single mother told me, with tears rolling down her cheeks, that her two boys would have not received anything for Christmas that year without the toys we gave them. I looked in the back seat of her car and the boys were brimming with happiness and excitement. That was one of the best moments of my year in 2020 and it came as a result of choosing to be a blessing. Every time I served at one of those outreach events, I experienced a peace and joy like no other. There is no greater satisfaction than knowing you had a positive impact on someone else's life for the glory of God.

Galatians 5:13-14 (Message) — *"It is absolutely clear that God has called you to a free life. Just make sure that you don't use this freedom as an excuse to do whatever you want to do and destroy your freedom. Rather, use your freedom to serve one another in love; that's how freedom grows."*

You can be a force for good. You can make a difference, and that is exactly what God wants you to do. Let me also say it is what you should do. We all should. We need more people who are determined to make the world around them a better place. God has given you peace for you to be a peacemaker. God has forgiven you for you to also forgive others. God has accepted you, so go be kind and accepting of others. Your life cannot only be free, but it can also help bring others into the same freedom you are experiencing. You can set the tone in your family for love, peace, generosity and integrity. In fact, Jesus made very clear in His teachings that all Christians are purposed to be the salt of the earth and the light of the world. The greatest way to be salt and light is by choosing to be a force for good. Do not just be blessed, but be a blessing. That is why the enemy promotes selfishness, compromise and dissention. That is why he wants you to be stuck in your past. That is why he tries so hard to keep you burdened and stressed out. He does not want your light to shine. He wants to keep you, and the people around you, separated from the goodness of God. The last thing Satan wants is for God to get glory from your life. That is why the enemy is determined to have you missing peace, but you know better now. You know you have been and will always be the recipient of God's peace. Now, you can share it. You can inspire others with it. You can help people by encouraging them and speaking life over them. Do not let the world flip the switch and turn your light off. Go be the amazing person God called you to be by showing people with your life just how incredible Jesus is. As you do, you will discover the fulfillment and satisfaction that comes when you know you have done something great.

84

■ Free to Live
4 Your Best Life

Maybe up to this point your life has not played out the way you thought it would. Maybe the mistakes of your past, the regret of those failures and the shame associated with it all has weighed you down and robbed you of your passions and expectations. Maybe you have fallen into the darkness of anxiety and depression and you feel like there is no more light. The enemy is trying to hold you back. He is constantly waging a war to contain and limit you, but you are free from it all. As you have read these first few chapters, you should now be forming a new sense of identity and expectation. 1 Thessalonians 1:4 says, *"God not only loves you very much, but also has put His hand on you for something special."* He is not finished with you yet. Your best days are not behind you. Your best days have not been withered away. Your best days are not over. Your best days are ahead of you. God has a wonderful life planned out for you.

You are free to chase your dreams.
You are free to hope once again.
You are free to be happy.
You are free to have a great expectation.
You are free to serve and love others.
You are free from your past.
You are free to live a great life.
You are free to take a stand.
You are free to enjoy the peace of God.

Now, go live your best life.

Shame No More

Shame No More

The Scarlet Letter, by Nathaniel Hawthorne, is an American classic. The narrator of the novel tells the story of the aftermath of an affair between the main character, Hester Prynne, and an unknown lover, later revealed as Reverend Arthur Dimmesdale. Hester had been sent from England to Boston by her husband to establish a new life while he wrapped up his business dealings before joining her in a new land. Time goes by and Hester's husband never makes it to Boston, or so she believes. In a moment of weakness, she and Dimmesdale have an affair from which Hester gets pregnant with her daughter, Pearl. The story begins with Hester being led from prison into the town square with her infant daughter in her hand and the Scarlett Letter "A" on her chest, to be admonished and punished for her adultery. Hester and her daughter go on to live ostracized and separated from their community. It takes years of good deeds on her behalf to earn even the smallest amount of respect and care from the people around her. This story reveals that Hester is a good woman who made a mistake, yet she is marked, identified and judged by that mistake her entire life. She lives tortured by her error and lack of judgment as a young woman far beyond reasonable expectation. Beyond what other people thought of her, the ultimate punishment came from within herself. She never escaped shame and self-condemnation.

As a young boy, I actually remember not liking this book as I read it on assignment for a book report in middle school. By no means is that a criticism of the author's writing. Obviously, it is one of the greatest literary accomplishments of all time. I just did not like the story itself. It never sat well with me. I remember thinking to myself that no one deserves to be ostracized or outcast like Hester was. I remember grieving for her, Pearl and Dimmesdale, who tortured himself until his eventual demise in the story. I was raised in a household of forgiveness so I just could not wrap my head around shaming someone for their entire life based on one moment of weakness or breakdown. Was there no forgiveness? Was there no redemption? Was there no opportunity to right a wrong? If you have read this book, you remember the depth of pain experienced not just by the main characters, but by the people around them as well. Where did that pain come from? Was it a result of the sin that was committed, or of the shame poured out in the aftermath of the sin? The answer is simple. The long-term pain the characters experienced came from the scarlet letter — the shame!

Shame is one of the most powerful and potentially destructive human emotions that one can experience. Living your life full of shame will have a significant, negative impact on the level of happiness you experience in your future – an impact that most do not comprehend and usually underestimate. Shame is that painful feeling arising from the consciousness of a mistake, sin or action deemed to be dishonorable. The world loves to shame people. Of course, they do not want to be labeled by shame themselves, but they sure do enjoy shaming others. In fact, the love of shame has produced what is now commonly referred to as cancel culture. That is exactly what shame aims to do — it wants to cancel your joy and peace. The cancel culture we are witnessing is wholly hypocritical though. Forgive me of my wrongdoing as I hold yours against you. Do not punish me for my sins while I give you the maximum sentence for yours. Jesus said it like this in Matthew 7:3: *"And why do you look at the speck in your brother's eye, but do not consider the plank in your own eye?"* In fact, the world loves to shame people so much, they have even created a cliché to use when someone messes up: "Shame on you," they say. Have you ever thought about that saying? What a damning statement. "Shame on you. I put shame on your life." Please don't ever say that to your children, and please don't say it to yourself. When we say that, we are claiming that the other person must now carry the pain and consciousness of their failures on their shoulders indefinitely. How awful is that? Jesus also said in Matthew 7:4, *"How can you say to your brother, 'Let me remove the speck from your eye;' and look, a plank is in your own eye?"* Shame is simply manmade judgment meant to keep people from experiencing freedom and forgiveness in their life. God told us that we are not the judge of humanity. We are here to love others and treat them like we prefer being treated. Let's not act the way the world acts. I encourage you to look at your own life, be accountable for it, make the changes you need to make, forgive others, forgive yourself, and move forward passionately pursuing the life you want to live. Please understand, if left unchecked, shame becomes a burden too heavy to carry. If you do not declare your freedom from it, shame will be the banner that hangs over your life. You must properly deal with this emotion or you will always return to the shame. It will become your scarlet letter. That is exactly what Hester Prynne did. After many years and even after Dimmesdale passed away, she left Boston with Pearl after removing the letter from her chest only to return sometime later with the "A" back on. For whatever reason, she did not have the internal fortitude to escape it permanently.

Shame robs you of life, joy and expectation. It torments you and produces a deep, internal struggle with guilt, grief and anger. It is a peace killer and a hope crusher. Shame is only focused on the past. Past mistakes. Past failures. Past sins. Past disappointments. Shame cannot exist without a living-in-the-past mindset. Romans 3:23-24 says, *"For all have sinned and fall short of the glory of God, being justified freely by His grace through the redemption that is in Christ Jesus."* Every one of us has things in our past that we would change if we could. The reality is, of course, that you cannot. And that is exactly why you must keep shame, regret, guilt and condemnation in their proper place, the past. You have been justified freely and set right by God's amazing grace. You are forgiven. With that said, I encourage you to not allow the errors of your past to carry more importance than they should. Do not elevate the hurt caused from your imperfection into a place of influence in your life that it does not deserve. I implore you not to exalt shame over God's forgiveness within your soul. At most, you should learn from past mistakes and disappointments so as to not repeat them – but that is where it should stop. Stop empowering the old version of yourself over the new version. Stop giving your past power over your present, enabling it to destroy your future.

89

Jesus made another powerful statement in verse 1 of Matthew 7 by saying, *"Judge not."* Far too often, we are our own harshest critic. I tend to do that to myself. Do you? The thing is, unless it produces change, it is not producing good. Why do we torment our own minds? Why do we punish ourselves beyond measure? You do not deserve to be judged by others, nor do you deserve to be judged by yourself. Why do we do this to ourselves? It is because we are taught early on in life that there must be consequence to our mistakes. This lesson is not wrong. Of course, there is consequence. For every action, there is in fact an equal and opposite reaction, but when handled incorrectly, this reality creates judgment and condemnation in our society. We learn to judge. We learn to punish. We learn to look for retribution. Talk too much in class, get detention. Drive too fast on the highway, get pulled over and receive a ticket. Be unfaithful to your spouse, probably get a divorce. From the time we are children, we are taught to feel remorse for the error of our ways. Remorse and shame are different emotions though. Remorse prompts change and restoration. Shame only produces guilt and regret. Maybe you have learned to judge yourself so harshly on a routine basis that you are gripped with guilt and regret. Here's the great news: if you learned something, that means you can unlearn it, or learn something new. You can learn to live without shame.

Psalms 4:1-2 — *"Hear me when I call, O God of my righteousness! You have relieved me in my distress; Have mercy on me and hear my prayer. How long, O you sons of men, will you turn my glory to shame? How long will you love worthlessness and seek falsehood? Selah."*

This is quite a revelation from David in his Psalm to his Chief Musician. You see here that God in His mercy and tender loving kindness relieves you from distress, yet many turn to shame anyway. You also see that shame produces a sense of worthlessness. I would hate for you to live that way. It is unnecessary and not God's will for you. God loves you so much that He sent Jesus to die on the cross for you to be a part of His family for eternity. No matter where you have been, no matter what you have done, and no matter how many times you have done it, God values you, believes in you and loves you unconditionally. You are not worthless; you are worthy of the love of God thanks to the sacrifice of Jesus on the cross! In the previous chapter about freedom, you read in Galatians where

"Whoever believes on Him will not be put to shame."

the Apostle Paul says to never again let anyone put a harness of slavery on you. That is exactly what the enemy wants shame to accomplish in your life. He does not want you free from distress. He wants you to declare allegiance to shame instead of loyalty to the freedom God has given you. He wants you to be enslaved to the pain of disgrace and worthlessness. All of it is designed to rob you of the peace of God. Please, do not let the favor and peace of God on your life be diminished by rejecting His mercy. You must understand in this moment that shame is a liar. Shame says because you failed, you are a failure. Shame says because you quit, you are a quitter. The lie of shame is that you are your mistake. Shame says, "Well, this is just who I am." If you believe these lies, you will live with a constant sense of unworthiness, self-judgment and self-loathing. Let me encourage you though: you are not your mistake, and you must begin to reject these terrible lies. Take the scarlet letter off of your chest. Be free from the pain of your past. Yes, maybe you failed, but you are not a failure to God and God will never fail you. Yes, maybe you quit, but you are not a quitter and God will never quit on you. Romans 10:11 says, *"Whoever believes on Him will not be put to shame."* There is no shame to those who believe in Jesus. The world says, "Shame on you," but Jesus says, "Shame no more." Praise the Lord!

91

Unlike Hester Prynne in *The Scarlet Letter*, your entire life does not have to marked by the mistakes you have made or the sins you have committed. You are loved and forgiven by God, no matter what. At this point, you understand that great reality, but that does not mean those mistakes do not still conjure up intense memories and feelings. To truly overcome the power of shame, you must be willing to recognize the internal and external emotions and experiences that led to it in the first place. If you are going to overcome, you have to acknowledge its existence. Denial never produces progress. Shame left to fester in your heart will only produce misery and torment.

It is the Law of Entropy in the world of emotions. To summarize, the Law of Entropy states that anything left unto itself will lead to disorder and decay. If you ignore a problem, the problem will only get worse. If you ignore a negative emotion within your heart, the emotion will only produce more negativity. That negativity will multiply to the point that the burden becomes far too heavy to carry. Jesus said, "Come to Me all who are burdened, and I will give you rest. For My yoke is easy and My burden is light." The burden of shame is a burden you do not have to carry any longer. God wants your life to flourish and to be blessed, but it will never become a reality if you will not put down the burden of shame.

Psalms 4:4-5 — *"Be angry, and do not sin. Meditate within your heart on your bed and be still.   -Selah*
Offer the sacrifices of righteousness and put your trust in the Lord."

It is quite clear from David's writing in this Psalm that he recognizes the need to address and control the negative emotion resulting from shame. In this instance, it is anger. Whatever it is though, be on guard to not allow damaging feelings resulting from failures to turn your heart toward self-condemning shame. Rather, make time to reflect on the mistake, learn from it, give it to God and move on. The ultimate goal of shame is to attempt to disqualify you. Here is how. Sin produces guilt. Guilt produces shame. Shame produces condemnation. Condemnation produces disqualification. The accusation of shame says that because you are flawed, you are unacceptable, but the truth of the grace of God says that though you are flawed, you are accepted and favored. That is why we are told to keep our trust in God and lean not on our own understanding. In these moments, the understanding of our own shortcomings will lead us to accept a false reality within our hearts. It is a reality that says you cannot serve God anymore, that you have done too much to receive the goodness of God, that you deserve to feel guilty, that you are disqualified from the promises of God. Eventually, you will disconnect from God, stop worshipping Him, quit going to church and be separated from His will for your life. If you allow this to happen, your life will stagnate or decay, and that is not what God wants.

The word 'blessed' in the Bible carries numerous definitions. One of them is "a life that always moves forward." The God of peace, of all blessing, has declared over you that no circumstance should be allowed to cause your life to languish and stop. You must move forward. The Bible says in Romans 8:1, *"There is therefore now no condemnation to those who are in Christ Jesus."* It also says there is no sin that can separate you from the love of God. Jesus did not come to condemn the world, but to save it. You are not condemned. You are not being judged by God. He is not angry with you. You have not fallen out of His grace. You have not done too much. Nothing can come between you and God's love, and that is why it is so important to uproot shame out of your heart and mind. Satan just wants to disqualify you from pursuing your God-given promises, but God declared peace and blessing onto your life and there is nothing anyone can do to remove it. God is not shame-focused, He is promise-focused! You are highly favored by Him and you are forgiven. In fact, God tells us in Romans 5:20, "Where sin abounds, grace (undeserved favor) abounds much more." Shame will always attempt to rule your emotions, but you do not have to let it.

Psalms 4:6-7 — *"There are many who say, 'Who will show us any good?' Lord, lift up the light of Your countenance upon us. You have put gladness in my heart."*

93

What an amazing chapter this is! You read here the "defeated" mentality of unbridled shame. *"Who will show us any good?"* David wrote that statement in the form of a question. Shame will cause you to say, "No one will show me any good." Once again, the lie of the devil is exposed. God is good. You may have not been good, but He still is. He is the author of good. He only produces good, and His good results in gladness, not sorrow or shame. You do not influence God; He influences you. **Shame is not what other people can do to you or say about you, rather, it is what you permit it to be.** Shame cannot be present within your soul unless you consent to its existence. From this moment forward, allow it to be removed from your life. Romans 5:17 states, *"For if by one man's offense death reigned through the one, much more those who receive abundance of grace and of the gift of righteousness will reign in life through the One, Jesus Christ."* Sin produces a defeated life. Righteousness produces a victorious one. That is why shame will always try to exalt sin over grace and righteousness, but all you have to do is reject shame and receive the gift God of favor and right standing that

Jesus gave you. Shame just wants you to reject the gift and accept the pain so you will live defeated and dominated by emotions that have no positive impact on your life. Grant yourself permission to receive the grace of God into your heart to empower you back into a place of joy. Who will show you any good? God will — not some of the time, but all of the time!

Psalms 4:8 — *"I will both lie down in peace and sleep. For You alone, O Lord, make me dwell in safety."*

A life given to God is a peace-filled life. There is no sin, no mistake, no failure and no accusation that can separate you from the peace God has for you. This reality is so important because it enables you to reshape the condition of your heart and refocus the mentality of your mind into one ruled by hope for your future. That is the mentality you are free to have. You do not have to be like Hester Prynne in *The Scarlet Letter*. You do not have to be ruled by shame, be identified by shame, or return to your shame like she did. God has not branded you with a letter on your chest to constantly remind you of the darkness of your past. This reality is truly one of the most freeing promises God has blessed us with as His children. I pray you are being encouraged and inspired by the truth laid out in this chapter. I hope you are allowing how you view yourself to be redefined. I pray the burden of shame has been lifted off your shoulders and there is now going to be a sense of ease in your life. You no longer have to weep at night and tear yourself apart over your mistakes and failures. You no longer have to tell the story of gloom and misery that ruled your past. You can write a new story, but this time it will be filled with love, joy, laughter and peace.

Let me show you one last amazing scripture before we move on to the next chapter. The scripture is Isaiah 61:7 (NLT) — *"Instead of shame and dishonor, you will enjoy a double share of honor. You will possess a double portion of prosperity in your land, and everlasting joy will be yours."* This is your promise from God. Not shame, but honor. Not lack, but prosperity. Not sorrow, but joy! Shame no more!

CHAPTER 8

In the Face of Disappointment

In the Face of Disappointment

If there is one thing we all have in common, other than the fact that we are imperfect and make mistakes, it is that every one of us will have to deal with disappointment at some point in our lives – probably more than once. Disappointment sometimes seems like it comes in seasons. In May 2012, my mother was diagnosed with stage 4 ovarian cancer. She died on December 30th of that same year. Those six months were brutal for our family. My mother was a spectacular woman. She was strong and bold in faith. She was a leader, a pastor, a friend and a role model. She was also the picture of health. She ate almost perfectly healthy food. She exercised five or six times per week. In fact, when I was in high school, she won a powerlifting competition. I used to be so embarrassed when she would ask me to work out with her. It is not an easy pill to swallow for a 17-year-old, testosterone-filled young man to watch his 110-pound mother lift more weight than him at the gym. Indulge me for a moment while I tell you her favorite story. We were at World's Gym in El Paso one day. There were two really big men doing a leg workout. They were finishing up on the leg press machine with about 500 pounds. That is a lot of weight for most anyone, but not for my mom. She routinely leg pressed over 600 pounds. She walked over and asked if they were done. They politely said yes and offered to remove the weight for her. I remember the huge smile on her face like it was yesterday as she told them, "No no, you can leave the weight. I'll use it to get started." She loved when I would tell that story. She would just laugh and laugh. Quite honestly, I could go on and on with stories of her physical discipline and strength, so needless to say, when the doctor's report of a football-sized tumor in her stomach and stage 4 cancer was spoken, we were in total and complete shock as a family.

After months of chemotherapy and various treatments, one day in November her lungs filled up with liquid and she began to severely struggle to breathe. We rushed her to the hospital. The emergency room doctor whispered to my dad they were not sure she would make it through the night. Her body was so stressed, the doctors were concerned she was going to have a heart attack. My sister Shannon and I stood with her as the nurses and doctors used their incredible talents and abilities to keep her alive. I remember grabbing her hand at one point only to see the desperation in her eyes as she mouthed the words "I love you" to me. My mom had a passion for life. She had every expectation she would overcome this disease and live to tell her testimony, so she fought, and she made it through the night; but, things were not good. We were in shock because the week before this happened, she had received what we thought to be a positive report and had been filled with hope that she was doing better. That weekend at Providence Memorial Hospital in El Paso was one of the worst weekends our family has ever experienced. We soon found out that the positive report was wrong, and in fact, her situation was far worse than any of us knew. As one of her doctors explained to us the cancer had spread to her lungs, I began to feel completely overwhelmed. The doctor left. I went to the restroom in the ICU waiting area. I remember leaning up against the wall, sliding down into a squatting position with my head buried in my hands and weeping for the first time since she had originally learned of her diagnosis. I would later describe it as feeling like I was caught in a current in the ocean being pulled out to sea. No matter how hard I swam, I could not get out of the current. Disappointment can feel that way sometimes. It can feel like the waves just keep crashing down on you, like the tide has come in and you are powerless in the face of it. It is difficult. It hurts. It is exhausting. It is overwhelming. At times, it can be crushing. Truly, disappointment is an attack on your life and your health.

Disappointment is defined as the frustration, defeat or failure of an expectation or hope. **The first thing you need to understand is that** disappointment is not from God. God does not disappoint. He is the God of fulfillment. He is the God of victory. He is the God of hope. In fact, Jesus is described as the hope for humanity. God is good and He only does good; therefore, you cannot associate disappointment with Him. The source of disappointment is Satan and humanity. The second thing you need to understand is disappointment comes in all shapes and sizes. A lost job. An abusive marriage. A divorce. A terrible car accident. A negative health report. A life-altering mistake made by one of your children. The reality is that disappointment and mourning has come, and it will come again into your life. The danger is not truly understanding its effect in your heart and mind, preventing you from properly dealing with it. Disappointment is one of the most dangerous, negative human emotions. Allowing it to fester and take root in your life can be incredibly destructive to your peace, hope and happiness. You must face it, deal with, and overcome it. And you can!

John 10:10 — *"The thief does not come except to steal, and to kill, and to destroy. I have come that they may have life, and that they may have it more abundantly."*

Satan wants nothing more than to use the hurt that comes from a frustration, defeat or failure of a positive expectation to rob you of the life God wants you to enjoy. I have even found that, often, right at the precipice of a new God-given opportunity, the enemy will try to knock people off track with a disappointing situation or circumstance. Why does this happen? The answer is simple. He wants you to give up and quit on your plans, your dreams and your vision for the future. He wants you to lose sight of the calling of God on your life. It has happened to me and my family numerous times. In 2007, our church was just about to finish a three-year construction project on a brand new 3,600 seat auditorium with amazing youth and kids' facilities, when the general contractor suddenly went bankrupt. As I mentioned previously, my wife and I lost a child to miscarriage. In 2012, my mother was diagnosed with cancer one month before my firstborn son was born. The enemy will attempt to attack the vulnerabilities of your heart and mind associated with these types of circumstances to bind you to the power of disappointment. His goal is to convince you to believe that your future has nothing to offer. If you accept this lie as truth, you will live in misery. No matter what has happened, remember that Jesus says He has a great future planned for you. Through all the tests, trials or failures, you must be determined not to give into the power of disappointment. Do not allow the abundant life to be stolen from your future due to past or current negative circumstances.

Every disappointing situation you find yourself in brings your life to a crossroads, and how you respond to it will determine the path your future takes. It will define your future joy and happiness. We spent several days in the ICU waiting room at the hospital my mom was in. As we were there, people began to recognize us. Word got out in the hospital, and consequently in the city. Church members who were nurses, doctors and therapists in the hospital began to find out we were there. One day my dad went to get a bottle of water from the vending machine around the corner from my mother's room. About thirty minutes later, he returned. I asked him what took him so long thinking maybe he just went for a walk to clear his head a bit. It would make perfect sense in that time that my dad would just need a moment to think and process everything that was going on. To my surprise, he told me he was down the hall praying for a hospitalized man whose wife recognized him when he went to get the bottle of water. I was so impressed. No matter how much pain he was in, he was still a pastor to that family. No level of distress or confusion was going to pull him away from what he was called by God to do. **You choose the path your life walks down. You determine if you will walk your future with or without God.**

Here's the question: are you going to be defeated by life and circumstance, or are you going to fight for your abundant life, fight for what is right, and fight for what God has planned for you? In every severely disappointing situation you find yourself in, you are in a fight. The enemy is coming after you, but you need to know — even the gravest situation should not be permitted to destroy you. The power of God is in you and Jesus has promised you victory over this world and the enemy. You must decide no matter what happens, you are going to be victorious. The night after my mom passed away, I was driving home from our church. I live in west El Paso, about thirty minutes away from the church in east El Paso. While I was driving on Interstate 10, I was having a very justifiable pity party within my mind. I was mad, hurting, angry and sad. As worship music played in the background, I began to pray and at one point, I cried out to God and said, "What are we going to do?" You see, my mom was not just a mom to me. She was the co-senior pastor of our church. She was the leader of our staff and volunteers. She was highly regarded as a visionary and beloved as a woman of compassion and dignity. I was unsure if our church would survive. It was an overwhelming time of confusion and fear, but God responded to me that night. When I got home, I wrote down word for word what the Lord said to me. He spoke these words, "You will turn to me in this time and I will give you peace. Like King David, you will rise from the ashes and carry on doing My work. Do not allow your disappointment to become anger or bitterness. Do not allow your hurt to lead to devastation. Your loss cannot become your ruin. I have placed too great a purpose on your family and on Abundant for you to quit now."

Your family, your friends, your coworkers, your church and your city need you to stand up and follow God down the right path — the path that leads to peace, healing and restoration. Disappointment left unchecked is the starting place of a toxic mindset. What do I mean by that? Disappointment leads to frustration. Frustration leads to anger. Anger leads to bitterness. Bitterness leads to envy, jealousy and strife. James 3:16 says, *"For where there is envy and strife, there is confusion and every evil thing."* The end result of disappointment is not a life you want to live. If left unchecked, insecurity, negativity, anxiety, hatred and depression will rule you. It is in these moments that you need strength, you need help, and you need encouragement. You must determine not to allow disappointment to lead to devastation. You are not devastated! The situation you went through may have been devastating, but you do not have to be. Please, do not allow your loss to become your ruin. You still have a life to live. A good life, filled with joy, satisfaction and purpose. God is not done with you yet.

In the first three months of 2013, after my mom went to Heaven, I was worn out. I was exhausted physically, mentally, emotionally and spiritually. My family was worn out. Our church was worn out, but we had a choice to make. Do we run from God, or do we run to God? The voice in my head told to me to run from God. I was upset. Why did my mom die at just 62 years old? She lived a healthy life.

Why didn't she get healed? Why didn't we discover the cancer in stage 1 or 2 so it could have been stopped? Questions abounded in my mind that logic told me I would not have answers for until it is my turn to go to Heaven. I still had a life to live though, a wife to love, a child to raise, a sister to be there for, a dad to support and a church to pastor. I had to remind myself, and I encourage you to do the same, of God's promises. I had to allow myself to remember all the good He had done for me. My mom died on Sunday, December 30th. We had our annual New Year's Eve service the following evening. The Nieman family went to church. I prayed for the church. My dad preached a message of hope and faith. We cried. We laughed. We worshipped. We did not run from God; we ran to God and He was there for us!

Looking back on everything we went through during 2012 and beyond, I realize now that the enemy was not just attacking my mother, he was attacking our entire family and our church. He wanted us to quit on our calling. He would have enjoyed nothing more than for my dad to determine he would never be happy again. The devil would have rejoiced if we had all just decided that was it, it was over, enough was enough. He would have loved for us to give in to the pain of disappointment and be defeated by it once and for all. Disappointment is one of the biggest and most persistent liars you will ever face. The problem is that the lies are within your own heart and mind. And let me tell you, those lies scream loud and they scream often.

Disappointment is a world of:

> It should have been.
> If only I had...
> Why didn't God...?
> Where was God when...?
> What if...?
> Where did my faith go wrong?
> Did I not pray enough?
> Everyone is against me.
> What's the use anyway?

"Draw near to God and He will draw near to you."

Please understand there is a war being waged on your thoughts during these seasons in an effort to drown out the voice of reason, logic, clarity, hope and wisdom. Ultimately, it is trying to drown out the voice of God in your life. Of course, this war is designed to keep you tormented and missing your promised peace. Psalms 46:10 says, *"Be still, and know that I am God."* One translation of this scripture says to step out of the noise and traffic of life so you can hear the voice of God. The attack on your thoughts is simply trying to build strongholds of defeat, failure and doubt in your mind. You cannot let that happen.

James 4:8 — *"Draw near to God and He will draw near to you."*

There is no greater investment you can make of your time and effort than to place them before God. You are invited by Him to go to Him in every situation, particularly the worst of them. The Bible says Jesus is your ever-present help in times of need. It also says when His people cry out to Him, He hears and responds. Jesus is near to those with a broken heart or a disappointed soul. The beautiful truth behind the above scripture in James is the act of drawing near to one another is not an equal transaction. It reads like it is, but it is not. You see, when you draw near to God, you do so in your ordinary self, but He draws near to you with His extraordinary power. You draw near to Him in your natural state, but He draws near to you in His supernatural glory. You draw near to Him with your sin, but He draws near to you with forgiveness. You draw near to God with your brokenness, but He draws near to you with healing and restoration. You draw near to him with anxiety, but He draws near to you with the peace which surpasses all understanding. You draw near to Him with confusion, but He draws near to you with wisdom and clarity. You draw near to Him with disappointment, but He draws near to you with hope. Whatever it is, wherever you are, however you may feel, you need to **run to God.**

103

In challenging and hurtful times, there is a human tendency to isolate into loneliness. In fact, many people will tell you to do just that as well. After my mother passed away, I cannot tell you how many people told me to take a sabbatical and go somewhere quiet. I remember thinking that was the last thing I wanted to do. I was already sad and grieving; I didn't really want to add lonely to the list of negative emotions I was experiencing. I went to work. I went to church. I went to the gym to exercise. I chose to live my life and it truly helped me accelerate the healing process. Eventually, Karla and I went on a nice trip to decompress, but not immediately. Isolation is incredibly dangerous; it is ultimately destructive to hold in your thoughts, feelings and emotions in times of failure, pressure or intense pain. You are not alone. God is with you. He never leaves you. He will always answer you. People are there for you too. It is amazing how ready people are to talk, listen and help when you reach out. If you feel like you have no one, go to your church or find a church, and you will find support. It is within these moments that disappointment truly challenges your resolve and determination. At some point, we all must decide we are going to persevere through the pain.

2 Corinthians 11:23-27 — *"Are they ministers of Christ? —I speak as a fool—I am more: in labors more abundant, in stripes above measure, in prisons more frequently, in deaths often. From the Jews five times I received forty stripes minus one. Three times I was beaten with rods; once I was stoned; three times I was shipwrecked; a night and a day I have been in the deep; in journeys often, in perils of waters, in perils of robbers, in perils of my own countrymen, in perils of the Gentiles, in perils in the city, in perils in the wilderness, in perils in the sea, in perils among false brethren; in weariness and toil, in sleeplessness often, in hunger and thirst, in fastings often, in cold and nakedness."*

Look at this list of challenges and disappointments the Apostle Paul faced and overcame. I am fairly confident when I say that no one reading this book will have a list quite like this. I can only imagine how discouraging this was for him. All Paul cared about was doing the work of God, and yet he faced so much opposition. He was beaten, shipwrecked, betrayed, lied about, tortured and robbed, yet he moved on anyway. He never allowed disappointment to rob him of the purpose of God on his life. Why? Because he knew that quitting made disappointment permanent. The Word of God says there is a time and a season for everything under the sun. The danger is to allow the bad times and seasons to last longer than they should. Hebrews 12:2-3 says in the New Living Translation, *"We do this by keeping our eyes on Jesus, the champion who initiates and perfects our faith. Because of the joy awaiting him, He endured the cross, disregarding its shame. Now He is seated in the place of honor beside God's throne. Think of all the hostility He endured from sinful people; then you won't become weary and give up."* There are certain times in life when you are going to have to decide to look to Jesus and fight the good fight of faith. Sometimes you may need to just take one more step, and then one more, and then one more until you get where you want to go. Occasionally, you may just have to pick yourself up off the floor, dust yourself off and keep moving forward. Whatever you do though, do not quit! When you are tempted to give up, ask yourself this question: will quitting make my life or this situation better? The overwhelming majority of the time, the answer will be no. Don't quit on your family. Don't quit on your life. Don't quit on God. Through Jesus, you have the endurance to push through the exhaustion, you have the strength to overcome the feeling of weakness, and you have the power of God to overcome the power of the world.

Proverbs 13:12 (Message) — *"Unrelenting disappointment leaves you heartsick, but a sudden good break can turn life around."*

This scripture truly highlights the importance and urgency of what I have been speaking to you about in this chapter. Unrelenting disappointment is pollution to your heart. If your physical heart is sick, your body does not function well. In fact, if it gets sick enough, your body will stop functioning altogether. The same is true of your passions, your desires, your expectation, and your hope. If you allow disappointment to stick around within you, your life will stop functioning. You will stagnate and never see your dreams come true. One translation of Proverbs 13:12 says, *"Hope deferred makes the heart sick."* And now we see the ultimate goal of disappointment is to become so unrelenting that you become hopeless. Of course, this makes perfect sense. Disappointment is the antithesis of hope. The enemy wants you to live a hopeless life. Hopelessness is a world of accepting inevitabilities, resigning to fate and living a faithless life. If you accept this as your reality, you will ultimately live a life of impossibilities.

It sounds like this:

> It's impossible for me to be happy again.
> It's impossible for me to go back to school.
> It's impossible for me to quit drinking.
> It's impossible for us to have a good marriage.
> It's impossible to overcome this depression.
> It's impossible to forgive what they did to me.
> It's impossible. It's impossible. It's impossible.

But it is not impossible. Those are the words of a sick heart spoken from a place of unrelenting disappointment.

Luke 1:37 — *"For with God, nothing will be impossible."*

There are two ways to read this scripture and both are correct. The first way is the most obvious way concludes with the reality that God can do anything. There is simply nothing He cannot do. He is all knowing and all powerful. He faces no impossibility. The second, less obvious way concludes with the reality that doing nothing is impossible to God. God cannot NOT work on your behalf. The Bible says He watches over His Word to perform it. It also says all His promises have been guaranteed as an inheritance for His children through a covenant between Him and man, sealed by the power of the Holy Spirit. If there is one thing that is actually impossible to God, it is doing nothing for you. As you read in Proverbs 13:12 that unrelenting disappointment will bring poverty to your soul, you also read that *"a sudden good break can turn life around."* The enemy wants you to be so consumed by the power of disappointment that you miss out on the sudden good break God has for you. Please do not let that happen. Keep your eyes open. Keep believing things can get better. Keep pursuing your passions and dreams. No matter how impossible it may feel, you serve the God of the impossible. If He said He will fight your battles for you, that is exactly what He is going to do. If He said He will deliver you, then deliverance is in your future. If He said He will pour out His blessing on you, get ready to be blessed. You see, the world wants to take you from hope to hopelessness, but God takes you from hope to fulfilled dreams and promises. This is why the word hopeless does not appear in the Bible. I once heard Pastor Bill Johnson from Bethel Ministries say, "Any area of your life that is hopeless is under the influence of a lie." There is no such thing as hopelessness when you are connected to the God of hope. There is no situation greater than the power of God. There is no bad circumstance that God cannot turn around. There is no pain God cannot heal. My prayer for you right now is while you read this chapter, God was igniting a new sense of excitement and expectation for your life. I pray He sparked a new hope for you.

107

Turning Disappointment Into Victory

THE MISSING PEACE

Turning Disappointment Into Victory

"Don't let go of your faith." Those six words changed my life. To this very moment, they reverberate in my mind. One morning in March of 2020, as word of city and nationwide shutdowns began to spread due to the COVID-19 global pandemic, I repeated those words to myself countless times as the enemy tried to overcome me with the prospect of our church being shut down, and with everything else going on around the world. Have you ever felt like you were losing your faith? Have you ever felt like there was just no hope anymore? Have you ever felt completely overwhelmed by life, circumstance, pain or hurt?

Faith is a vital spiritual tool for your mental and emotional health. It helps you enjoy the amazing life God wants you to have. It is truly a gift from the Lord, but it is also something you choose and must fight for. Faith is the overcoming power of the kingdom of God that brings the enemy and the world into a place of defeat. 1 John 5:4 shows us faith in God is what gives us the victory over the world. You have been given this power by God to use at your disposal to overcome all challenges and obstacles life may bring your way. The reality is life will sometimes try to crush you. Please understand though, that is not something to be afraid of. It is just something to be remember. In fact, as a child of God, you actually have nothing to fear. Fear is a liar. It is a myth, a mirage. Fear is nothing more than a deceptive circumstance or consequence posing as something that can overcome you. It cannot! The appearance of fear in your life arrives to intimidate you into believing you are not capable of doing what God has called you to do. Fear is False Evidence Appearing Real. The Bible tells you to not be afraid exactly 365 times. Do you think that is a coincidence? Absolutely not. The only option Satan has to try to defeat you is to fool you with fear into believing something contrary to God's Word.

> "There's no way I can do that."
> "I am not strong enough to get through this."
> "I am too broken to ever be happy again."
> "No one in my family has ever accomplished that."
> "I am too depressed. I am too anxious. I am too overburdened."

Statements like those are learned declarations of fear. Research has shown humans are only born with two fears: the fear of falling and the fear of loud noises. Both those fears are God-given for natural survival. Scientists have identified over 2,000 other phobias and fears, all of which are learned. As you mature in life, you learn to fear. You learn about panic. You learn about anxiety. You are told you should be afraid of certain people, places or things. The good news is if you learned something, you can unlearn it or learn something new. **Standing between you and the life you want to enjoy is fear.** You must overcome fear, and you do that with faith. Fear says you are defeated. Faith says you are victorious. Which declaration are you going to believe?

1 Peter 5:8 — *"Be sober, be vigilant, because your adversary the devil walks around like a roaring lion, seeking whom he may devour."*

It is vitally important when you read scripture to pay close attention to wording. Notice the phrases *"like a roaring lion"* and *"whom he may devour"* in the above scripture. Several years ago, I was blessed to travel with my dad on a ministry trip to South Africa. In between various speaking engagements at some incredible local churches, we found out we had a couple days off. To our delighted surprise, one of the pastors had booked us all to go on safari to see the wild animals of Africa. What a dream come true! I have been fascinated with Africa and its natural habitat my entire life. To this day, I record

Big Cat Week on the National Geographic Channel. From the moment the pastor told us about the trip, there was nothing more I wanted to see than an adult male lion. Filled with excitement and exhilaration, I woke up on the first morning of the trip before my 4:30 a.m. alarm went off. I was ready to go and it was everything I had ever imagined. The beauty, the calm, the sunrise over the African landscape was breathtaking. And then came the animals. We saw crocodiles, hippos, an assortment of birds, and much more. At one point, a mother giraffe and her baby came within 15 feet of our open-air Jeep. The mother checked us out with curiosity and caution, her baby always behind her to keep it protected. You may know the rhinoceros is almost extinct in the world, so it was such a thrill to drive up to a group of four of them grazing in an open field. We came so close to a herd of elephants that I could have literally reached out of our vehicle and touched them.

We saw just about everything, but we had not seen a lion. Honestly, I would have traded seeing all the other animals to just have that one moment. I even began to pray. I reminded God that He said He would give me the desires of my heart. Not sure if that was scripturally relevant or accurate when applied to that situation, but it was worth a shot. You have not because you ask not, right? We drove and drove, but still no lion. As we headed back to the lodge for lunch, I overheard "Tao, Tao, Tao" on our driver's radio. For some reason, I just knew it meant "lion." He turned around and asked us if we wanted lunch or were willing to continue the tour for an extra 30 minutes to go find our Tao. I screamed, "Yes," without hesitation and without consulting the rest of the people in our group. Off we went. I will never forget the moment the driver pulled around a huge tree and large collection of bushes. There they were in the thick grass: a full-size male and a full-size female lion, only about fifty yards away from me. My heart was bursting with joy! I took countless pictures and video. I was like a young kid walking up to the entrance of Disneyland for the first time. To my surprise though, the lions got up and began to walk toward our vehicle. My God, what an encounter! First, the female stepped into the path of our vehicle, only about fifteen feet in front of us, paused, looked at us and kept walking. Then came the male in all his splendor. You could see the confidence he had. He was the king of the land; he stood on. He had no rival, no equal and nothing to fear. As his mane waved

111

in the breeze, he stopped in the path as if to pose for the camera. I honestly believe God just gave me this moment. He made this dream of mine come true. It was something I will never forget. My dad and I still reminisce about him just standing there for about ten seconds, looking at us, looking at the female, and just looking around as if to say, "You see me and I see you."

The male lion I saw that day was strong and bold. It is easy to understand he lived to protect his pride. By force and intimation, he would defeat his enemies, and that explains why the devil goes around "like a lion." He wants you to be intimidated. He wants you to believe he is king. He wants you to accept that you are defeated. Let me tell you though, there is a lion in the Bible, but it is not the devil. The lion in the Bible is the lion of the tribe of Judah. The lion in the Bible is Jesus Christ. He is the King of Kings and the Lord of Lords, and He carries the name that is above every other name. When Jesus died on the cross, He defeated the devil and took all his power and authority away from him. That is why the enemy uses fear as his weapon of choice. If you accept fear, you accept the wrong power into your life. You begin to believe the wrong things. You will speak negativity, pain and ruin over your future. James 4:7 says, "Resist the devil and he will flee from you." Well, isn't that easy? You do not have to fight the devil. Jesus already fought and won that fight. You do not have to overcome the devil. Jesus already overcame him on your behalf. All you have to do is resist, and he will flee from you. 1 Peter 5 said he is seeking whom he may devour. My response to that is, no, you may not! This needs to become your attitude as well.

"No, you may not control my life. No, you may not destroy my family. No, you may not keep me depressed. No, you may not torment me with fear and anxiety. No, you may not have control of my heart and mind. No, you may not!"

One of the most challenging moments you will face in life is when it is time to resist the devil in the midst of unrelenting disappointment. In these moments you are most likely feeling weak, tired, overwhelmed and maybe even afraid. Your future is under attack. Our reference scripture in 1 Peter says, *be sober, be vigilant.* This is simply God telling us to pay attention and be aware of what the enemy is trying to accomplish. You must be on guard to what is taking place in these challenging seasons. The devil knows he cannot defeat you, so he tries to wear you down in an attempt to get you to stop resisting him. His goal is to take you from disappointment to defeat. The enemy wants you to accept a miserable life, a depressed life, a defeated life; but you are not going to do it. You now understand the game being played, but more importantly, you know you are going to win the game. You are a child of God and a child of faith. You are a child of the victorious God and victory has been laid out for your life. Please understand God can take any circumstance the enemy meant for evil and turn it for your good. You are not going to go from disappointment to defeat. You are going to go from disappointment to victory.

Turning Disappointment Into Victory:

■ The Courage
1 to Change

This may be the most difficult challenge you face during this process. Quite often, the disappointment in our lives is simply a result of our bad decisions, foolish behavior or toxic surroundings. We want new results without embracing new behavior. Change is hard. Change is challenging. Change is uncomfortable. People tend to resist change because their routines and habits are so familiar and easy to them, even if they are not happy with the results they produce. Over and over during his three years of ministry on the earth, Jesus told us to have courage, to fear not and to remove sin and wrongdoing out of our lives. **One small act of courage can change your life.** One moment of being bold can empower you to face and overcome fear so the entire trajectory of your future can change direction. Do you have the courage to change?

I believe the key to powerful and long-lasting change is self-accountability. Self-accountability is the willingness and determination to examine your life and take full and complete responsibility for it without having to be counseled or confronted by outside parties. It is the realization that I am 100% in control of my life, and I am responsible for making sure my life is headed in the right direction. Let's tell the truth though, accountability has basically become a four-letter word in today's society. It almost seems like no one wants to be held accountable for their actions or their words anymore. We make excuses. We blame anyone and everyone but ourselves. We blame God, the republicans, the democrats, our parents, our bosses, our friends or our situation in general. We tend to just find the easiest person or place to project our problems onto so we do not have to face the reality of the situation ourselves.

I have found that the most successful people I have ever been around have this one thing in common: they are self-accountable. As the saying goes, you cannot keep repeating the same behavior over and over again while expecting different results. Nothing changes if nothing changes. In order to build the life of success you really want, you must be willing to ask and answer, truthfully and continuously, the following three questions of self-accountability:

(1) What am I doing right?

(2) What am I doing wrong?

(3) What can I do better?

These questions are designed to force you to face the facts about your life and make the necessary changes for improvement. You can do it! It may not be easy at first, but it will be worth it. I run them through my mind constantly about my health, my marriage, our church, my kids, and even minor interactions and meetings. Having practiced this for years, I have found that answering those questions leads to three more questions that need to be answered.

(1) Is my focus on the right things?

(2) Are my surroundings healthy?

(3) Are the people I have allowed into my life building me up?

If your answer is 'no' to any of those questions, you have successfully identified what you need to change. Now, go start making the changes. Don't wait. Don't procrastinate. Don't blame other people. Don't make excuses. Take ownership of your life right now, in this very moment, so you can enjoy the future you have dreamed of. Have the courage to make the changes you know you need to make. You may have to face fears. You may have to get out of your comfort zone. You may have to overcome personal challenges. You may have to take steps of faith that seem risky. You may have to forgive or ask for forgiveness. At times, it will be hard, but it will always be worth it. Remember, God is on your side and you shall not be defeated. God is for you. You can do this. You must do this. You need to do this. If not now, when?

2 Put Your Trust in God

The first area of your soul the enemy will attack in extremely challenging or disappointing seasons is your trust, particularly your trust in the Lord.

Proverbs 3:5-6 — *"Trust in the Lord with all your heart, and lean not on your own understanding; in all your ways acknowledge Him, and He shall direct your paths."*

We clearly see from these scriptures the importance of keeping our trust in God. Upon doing so, you are immediately placed on His path, where He has promised to lead and guide your ways. The obvious challenge is overcoming the natural tendency to question everyone and everything when things have not gone your way. One of the most prevalent fears we learn is the fear of having our trust broken. Having trust issues is a self-defense mechanism born from past hurts and disappointments. From the pain of those events, people will put walls up within their hearts to protect against being hurt once again. The problem is you are keeping yourself from experiencing truly healthy, wonderful relationships. The fear of being hurt robs you of being happy. With that said, the greatest danger is to begin to question or not trust God. Disappointment is an assault on your trust. If the enemy can cause you to lose your trust in God, he can take your life down a very dangerous road.

I think it is safe to assume all of us have had our trust broken at some point in life. Maybe you were lied to by a friend. Maybe a boss manipulated and used you as a pawn to promote their own agenda, at your expense. Maybe you were cheated on. Maybe you were the victim of a business deal gone awry. You thought something was going to go one way, and it went the complete opposite way. These moments are difficult and often very hurtful, which is exactly why you must keep your entire trust in God, and not man. Man will always fail and disappoint, but God never fails. You need to keep yourself walking on His path, because it is His path that leads you to peace and happiness. A path of distrust leads to cynicism, suspicion and skepticism. That is not a path of peace.

A friend of mine called me several years ago to ask me to pray with him to get a promotion that he was next in line for at his company. His direct supervisor, who was the person leaving and creating the open position, had told him he had even recommended my friend for the job. He interviewed and was told everything went great, only to find out a week or so later that the head of his division had given the job to a person far less qualified than him. He was devastated, and even began searching for a new job himself. He called me so disappointed. All of his hard work, diligence and commitment to doing things the right way seemed worthless now. I told him to continue to trust God and we were going to believe together that God would open a great new door for him. Unfortunately, this was taking place during the recession of 2008, so new jobs were scarce. About six months passed and my friend showed up to work on a Friday morning only to be met by the FBI at the entrance of his office building. As he found out, the boss and the person he had promoted were committing some pretty serious crimes and were arrested that day along with several other people within the division. My friend had nothing to do with it and no knowledge of what had taken place. After the dust settled, guess who got promoted? My friend! We now both believe God was simply protecting him from even being associated with those people only to then give him an even greater position than he had originally applied for, with better pay.

Please understand that trusting God means you will not always understand everything taking place in the moment, but you can walk confidently knowing God is going to work out great things on your behalf. I have always found in extreme times of having to only rely and trust God that once He gets me where He intended for me to go, I look back and completely understand what took place. It is a matter of trusting God with all your heart, leaning not on your own understanding, and acknowledging Him in all your ways. This challenge of surrendering our trust and action to him can be so difficult, but ultimately, it is incredibly rewarding.

Jeremiah 17:7-8 — *"Blessed is the man who trusts in the Lord, and whose hope is the Lord. For he shall be like a tree planted by the waters, which spreads out its roots by the river, and will not fear when heat comes; but its leaf will be green, and will not be anxious in the year of drought, nor will cease from yielding fruit."*

Where is your trust? Is it in the Lord, or you have learned to put your trust in the wrong places? If it is not in God, it is time to make that change. Don't live your life with "trust issues" like so many people do. Look at what God wants to do for you when you trust Him. You may remember one of the definitions of the word "peace" refers to God blessing you. It is no coincidence that peace from God and trust in God are connected. Of course they are. When your trust is broken, it is easy to lack peace. The word "blessed" literally means to be enviably happy and to have a life that moves forward. It is much easier to be happy when your trust is in God because you know beyond a shadow of a doubt things are going to work out. You know He is going to bless your life. You may have to wait, but you always know His timing is the right timing. You may not understand the way, but you always know His ways are the right ways. Your thoughts may confuse you, but you always know His thoughts are the right thoughts. What is your job here? Keep your trust in Him.

The above scripture in Jeremiah is really quite astounding in another regard. It speaks of heat and drought, but it also speaks of green leaves and bearing fruit. This is clearly referencing the supernatural power and provision of God's favor being on your life during difficult times. In fact, when you look up the word "heat" in the original Hebrew dictionary, it means disappointment. So, God is telling you even when you are disappointed, if you will continue to trust Him, your life will continue to produce, move forward, expand and grow. The enemy wants you to give in to fear and anxiety, but the peace of God and your trust in God will turn the situation around. Keep your trust in God and allow Him to turn your disappointment into victory.

3 ◼ Don't Let Go of Your Hope and Faith

My mother was transferred from Providence Memorial Hospital in El Paso, where she fought for her life that weekend, to the world-famous M.D. Anderson Cancer Center in Houston, Texas. Her diagnosis was grim, but we had hope, nonetheless. She was at the premier cancer institute in the world, surrounded by the best doctors and facilities one can find. But our hope did not remain. I will never forget the night I overheard her doctor tell my dad, "I'm going to do everything I can, but this will be her last Christmas." I kept it to myself. I did not tell my wife, my sister or my dad I heard that report. I didn't need to. We all knew it without the doctor having to confirm it. I was raised on faith though, and I was going to believe with all my heart God could heal her for as long as she still had breath in her lungs. No matter what the report was, I was going to speak life and healing over my mom's body. You see, faith is a mountain mover. Faith is a world shaker. Faith is God's game changer, and it is His gift to us to live by. As His children, our way of life is faith. We are to continuously and unwaveringly believe and speak what God says and has declared over our lives. We walk by faith and not by sight. Faith overcomes fear. Fear cannot stand up to faith. Fear cannot stand up to faith because fear is founded on lies, while faith is founded on truth. The truth sets you free. When truth is applied to a lie, the lie unravels; therefore, when you apply faith to fear, fear unravels as well. Romans 10:17 says, *"So then faith comes by hearing (understanding), and hearing by the word of God."* Just as you learn fear, you learn faith. The more you know the goodness and promises of God, the more your faith expands within your soul. The more faith you know, the less fear you will have.

Hebrews 6:18-20 (Message) — *"We who have run for our very lives to God have every reason to grab the promised hope with both hands and never let go. It's an unbreakable spiritual lifeline, reaching past all appearances right to the very presence of God where Jesus, running on ahead of us, has taken up His permanent post as high priest for us, in the order of Melchizedek."*

Why does God tell you to grab the promised hope with both hands and never let go? Well, I already showed you that hope deferred or unrelenting disappointment will make your heart sick, but beyond that it will rob you of your faith and keep you bound to fear. Hebrews 11:1 says, *"Faith is the substance of things hoped for."* Hope and faith are divinely connected. Without hope, faith has nothing to do. The devil wants you to become a prisoner to disappointment, to a negative expectation, to anxiety. God wants you to become a prisoner to hope, to a positive expectation, to faith, to peace. **No matter what you may be facing, do not give up your positive expectation of God in your life.** He is faithful and just to watch over His promise-filled Word to perform it in your life. The entire plan of disappointment is designed by Satan to get you to let go of your hope, step out of faith, and live in fear. Whether you realize it or not, the moment you let go of hope, you are also letting go of faith. When you let go of faith, you are letting go of your promised victory.

ROMANS 4:18

"...who, contrary to hope, in hope believed."

A few nights after I overheard what the doctor told my dad, he and I went down to the hospital cafeteria late in the evening to get a snack. Everything was closed except the freezer with pints of Ben and Jerry's ice cream in it. My dad and I sat down, ate our ice cream and talked quietly about what was going on. At one point, he got up to go get some napkins. As I looked across the cafeteria, I heard what I believe was the Lord tell me inside my head, "Don't let go of your faith." In the moment, I thought God was referring to my mom and her battle with cancer. Looking back, I realize He was not talking about my mom. He was talking about me. When He spoke those words to me, He already knew three weeks from that night, she would be in Heaven, standing in His throne room, worshipping and praising His glory and majesty. He knew her time on earth was coming to an end. I was determined to have faith for her no matter what, but God's words to me were not about my mother, but about my future. I later realized He was reminding me that I still had a life to live. He still had a plan for me and my family. God was telling me that I could not allow this horribly devastating season to rob me of my faith in Him. He was telling me not to let go of hope, not to lose my trust in Him, not to become discouraged, and not to fear the future because of the failure of the past. So, I tell you now, no matter what you have gone through and no matter what you may face in your future, do not let go of your faith. Not now, not ever.

Romans 4:18 — *"...who, contrary to hope, in hope believed."*

This scripture in Romans is talking about Abraham, who is referred to as the Father of Faith. If you do not know the story, Abraham and his wife were unable to have children as they advanced in age. God promised him He would give him a son, but they were both far beyond the years of fertility and giving birth. In the natural sense, it seemed hopeless. These are powerful words though: "contrary to hope, in hope believed." There are times in life that things will appear completely hopeless, yet God says, keep believing anyway. Sometimes, you may only have the choice to put your faith in hope itself. Just believe something positive is going to happen. Your setback does not have to be permanent. You must resist the urge to become hopeless. You must resist fear. You must resist the lie of the enemy that you are being defeated. You are not overcome; you are an overcomer through faith. Do not give up. Keep believing. Never let go of your hope or your faith and watch God turn your disappointment into victory!

The Power of Vision

The Power of Vision

Having a clear and concise vision for your life is vitally important to your mental, emotional and spiritual well-being. As we have discussed in this book thus far, there is so much power in overcoming your past and moving toward a Godly future. Establishing your life's vision will play a major role in overcoming disappointment, pushing through seasons of obstacle, and pressing through the human tendency to stagnate. Habakkuk 2:3 says, *"Write the vision and make it plain on tablets, that he may run who reads it. For the vision is yet for an appointed time; but at the end it will speak, and it will not lie. Though it tarries, wait for it; because it will surely come, it will not tarry."* This is a powerful, important and famous scripture for many reasons. One reason is because it highlights the fact there is always Godly vision for your life. God restores, inspires and expands His vision continuously. He has more vision for your life than you can ever imagine. Therefore, the question becomes, "Do you?" Do you have a vision for your life and for your future? What about the specific areas that make up your life? You will see in this chapter why it is so valuable to have a defined vision for your marriage, how you want to raise your children, your physical health, your finances, your career and beyond.

A vision is defined as a vivid, imaginative conception or anticipation of things to come. Ephesians 3:20 in The Message translation says, *"God can do anything, you know, far more than you could ever imagine or guess or request in your wildest dreams!"* You and I serve an amazing God. He is extraordinary on every level. When we begin to receive and pursue a Godly vision, extraordinary things begin

"Where there is no vision, the people perish."

to happen. God wants to exceed your greatest plans. He desires for you to live a grand life, filled with passion and excitement. He gave you dreams with every intention of helping you see them be fulfilled, but in truth, He even wants to take you beyond that. He wants to do exceedingly, abundantly and above anything you can ever ask or desire. He is a big God, with big blessings, and He has a big plan for your future. You cannot underestimate the power of having a vision for your life. I am incredibly blessed to have been raised by visionaries. Our church has been led for more than forty years by a powerful vision God gave my parents to teach people how to enjoy the abundant life Jesus came to give them. I have never lacked for vision being spoken over my life. My mom used to pray over me at night as a child. After every prayer, she would tell me, "You are called and anointed by God to preach the gospel." Let me tell you, no matter who you are, no matter what your background is, no matter your age or personal situation, it is never too late to grab onto a God-inspired vision for your future. Once you do, your future will unfold in an incredible way.

A common theme I have experienced with people struggling to find peace in my years of pastoring and counseling is a sense of not having direction and focus in their lives. Quite often, the overwhelming presence of anxiety, depression or overburden makes them feel like they do not know what they are doing in life or where they are going. Proverbs 29:18 says, *"Where there is no vision, the people perish."* What an important scripture this is. You already know God wants your life to prosper and to be filled with peace and joy. He does not want you to perish. If you flipped this scripture from the negative to the positive, you could easily say where there is vision, the people thrive. That is what it's all about. In fact, that is what God is all about. God wants you to thrive, and He will do everything He can to see your life succeed, flourish and blossom on every level. Vision is important for many reasons, and

124

one of those reasons is it gives your life direction. Knowing where you are going in your future is invaluable to your peace of mind because it gives you clarity within your daily decision making and goal setting. With the overload of information being thrown at us daily via the internet, 24-hour news channels and social media, finding clarity of what is right and true can be so challenging. That is why God said to write the vision down and make it plain. Make it simple and make sure you can see it. Why? So you can run with it. You know exactly what you are doing and where you are going. One of the definitions of the word "perish" from the above scripture in Proverbs means people are scattered as wanderers or are like wild horses roaming aimlessly in fields. If you are scattered or wandering aimlessly, the direction of your life can be influenced by the wrong people or things, but when you have a vision, your life has intent, focus and purpose. Purpose empowers your mind to focus on the right people and things, while filtering out the wrong ones, the distractions.

As I entered my 30s, I began to struggle quite a bit with my eyesight. I have worn glasses and contacts since I was in high school, but something had begun to change. I slowly started noticing my vision was beginning to blur. Without my contacts on, I could not decipher anything other than large objects, much less read a book or watch television. After about eighteen months of decline, I went for my annual eye exam and was diagnosed with a condition called Keratoconus. This condition is one in which the clear tissue on the cornea bulges forward. Your cornea becomes shaped like a cone, hence the name, instead of being rounded. The two major symptoms of Keratoconus are blurred vision and sensitivity to light. I had both. My local eye doctor told me there was nothing I could do. He informed me, rather casually too, I would eventually be legally blind. I remember thinking he had to be wrong. Seriously! If we can put a man on the moon, there must be someone in America who can help my eyesight. After a significant amount of research, I found an incredible doctor in Beverly Hills, California named Dr. Brian Boxer Wachler. He is world renowned for creating a procedure that stops the progression of this condition, and sometimes even reverses it. I submitted all my information and was so excited to be accepted as a patient for his treatment. Since Keratoconus is so rare, people asked me all the time what

125

it is like. The best way I can describe it is like being in a fog. You can see, but you can't see.

1 Corinthians 13:12 in The Message Translation says, *"We don't yet see things clearly. We're squinting in a fog, peering through a mist. But it won't be long before the weather clears and the sun shines bright! We'll see it all then, see it all as clearly as God sees us, knowing Him directly just as He knows us."* Have you ever felt that way in life? I can see, but I just can't see. That is what lack of vision does to you. It is like you are peering through a mist. There is no clarity of direction and focus, but a God-given vision changes all of that. Vision is like the sun shining brightly through the fog. After my procedure was complete, the doctor's orders were for me to sit in a dark room for twelve hours straight with my eyes closed as much as possible. Naturally, I fell asleep. The next morning, I woke up anxious. Did it work? Would I be able to see? Did my body reject the procedure and blindness was in my future? I turned the light on in the hotel bathroom while slowly and nervously opening my eyes. I could see clearly! Not perfect, but way better than the day before. Life is so much better when you have clarity. Decision making is easier. Stress levels go down. Worry subsides. Anxiety is far less prevalent. The agony of what to do and the consequences therein are truly burdensome, but a clear vision relieves that burden.

In all my years of spending time talking to people, trying to help them and counsel them as they navigate the storms of life and the challenges they are facing, one of the things I have had repeated to me many times is the phrase, "I just don't know why I am here." The first thing I ask when I hear that statement or something like it is, **"What vision do you have for your life?"** Your vision defines why you are doing what you are doing. In fact, it will actually determine what you are doing, and even when to do it. One of the greatest benefits of having a powerful, vivid and clearly communicated anticipation for your future is it gives your life meaning. A dynamic vision will always give you reason to live, and it will add such great significance to your daily life. When I was 15 years old, we hosted a weeklong conference at our church. At the time, it was called The Spring Faith Convention. Pastors and delegates traveled from around the world to attend, to worship, to preach and to share their callings with the members of our church and our local community.

The church was packed into overflow every night for five nights in a row. A man named Tommy Barnett was the pastor scheduled to preach the last night of the conference. He had never visited El Paso before, but he and my father had developed a close, personal friendship. I will never forget how I felt as he shared a message called *The Miracle Is In The House*. At the end of the service, Pastor Barnett asked for people to come to the altar at the front of the church to seek God for how they could be the miracle in their house. Hundreds of people flooded the stage to pray, including me. As he continued to minister, I closed my eyes and there it was. I saw the future of my life. I saw a stage that had been placed at the top of the mountain range that El Paso is built around. I could see myself preaching God's Word to thousands and thousands of people. At that very moment, I knew my future was to pastor our church. My vision was set. My purpose was clear. Yes, I ran from it for years as I went through high school and college, but I could never shake that vision. I knew my life was attached to something greater than myself, and that is the beauty of a God-inspired vision for your future.

When vision grabs hold of your life, you immediately begin to recognize the potential to go beyond ordinary and accomplish something extraordinary. The excitement of your possibilities then becomes the focus of your thoughts and plans. You previously read that where vision does not exist, people are scattered. Why is that? People tend to scatter because they do not have boundaries. Having a powerful plan you are pursuing automatically places the necessary and coinciding boundaries in your life to fulfill those plans. When you know where your life is going, you make decisions accordingly. It is much easier to make the small, sometimes seemingly meaningless daily decisions and even far less stressful to make the major life decisions when you have a strong, God-inspired vision for your life. Quite often, you will not even have to pray about the choices you are faced with. It works like this: **if it does not fit within my vision, I don't do it.** I have a vision to have a marriage ruled by love, honor and respect, therefore, I do not yell, scream and lose my temper with my wife – no matter what. End of story. I have a vision to raise children to serve God, therefore, my kids go to church every week (even when they do not want to go), we pray before they go to sleep, we read the Bible together, and we teach them about generosity, faithfulness and integrity. A few years ago, my wife and I had a vision to build a house, so we took shorter vacations, bought all our clothes on sale, and cooked at home most evenings instead of going out to dinner. We did this for years so we could save money and prepare to watch our dream come true. It took a long time. It took some sacrifice. There were times when one of us wanted to splurge or even go in another direction, but we didn't. We held ourselves and each other accountable to the plan, the goal and the vision. And that really is the blessing of having a vision for your life. You are not scattered or wandering aimlessly through life being ruled by trends or feelings. Quite the contrary. The parameters, the boundaries and the course of your short-term and long-term decision making is already set. A vision simplifies life significantly while also allowing for simplistic accountability to exist. You do not have to fight, stress or overthink. If it does not fit the vision, we do not do it.

Psalms 37:4-5 — *"Delight yourself also in the Lord, and He shall give you the desires of your heart. Commit your way to the Lord, trust also in Him, and He shall bring it to pass."*

Part of the reason vision is so valuable to your life is because it tends to have self-fulfilling capacity, particularly when you commit what you are doing to God. When your plan is submitted to Him, He empowers you with His wisdom, provision and grace. There is simply no stopping the will of God in your life when you seek Him as your true leader and follow Him along the way. Remember, His will for you is to live in peace. It is God's desire and intent to direct you into a life of health, welfare, prosperity and every kind of good. What you must realize is He does not give you a dream with the intention of not helping you see the dream come true. Your vision, your dream, your plan was inspired by God for it to become your reality. Obviously, you must address it. You must pay attention to it. You must work hard at it. You must be determined to do whatever you need to do for it to be realized. You must protect it and take care of it. You cannot just leave it to itself and expect it to come to pass. As the scripture above says, *"Commit your way to the Lord, and He shall bring it to pass."* A Godly vision will always produce Godly behavior. Godly behavior always produces Godly results. Godly results produce a life you want to live. God inspires the vision, and He will deliver the results. What you need to do is act.

A car cannot get you where you need to go if you never take it out of the garage. The Bible says in the book of James that faith without corresponding action is dead. Life simply does not work any other way. You get out of life what you put into it. You reap what you sow; therefore, allow the boundaries of your life to guide you into the life you desire to live, and adjust your actions accordingly. This seems too obvious though, does it not? The problem is we humans tend to resent boundaries. We view them as restrictive and constraining, when in fact, they are often quite empowering. Think of it like a highway. A highway is literally designed to get you where you need to go. Within a highway's design are clearly defined boundaries and limits. We call them lanes and speed limits. Let me ask you a question: are those lanes and speed limits created to restrict you or to protect you? Now, your sarcasm may have led you to answer you sure feel restricted by slow drivers, but the truth is without those lanes and speed limits, the freeway would turn into chaos. Those boundaries actually create order, and the order helps you get to your desired destination safely and efficiently. The same is true with your vision. Give it to God, follow His ways, live accordingly, and He will get you where you want to go.

129

Several years ago, a friend of mine was going through an incredibly difficult season in his life. He battled depression, was diagnosed as bipolar, had a business that was failing, and was going through a divorce. We were new friends, so I was not completely aware of everything he was dealing with when he came to see me one Monday at my office. After a months-long battle, he had just been awarded sole custody and complete legal control over his two young daughters. He did not need to tell me he was overwhelmed. I could see it on his face. As happy as he was that his daughters would be with him, he was also terrified, hurting, and exhausted both mentally and emotionally. We talked for a while with my intent being to just listen to him and encourage him as much as I could. Toward the end of our conversation, he said, "What do I do with my daughters? I don't know how to raise little girls." I remember thinking to myself, "Why are you asking me?" I did not have kids of my own at that point. I told him to close his eyes. I asked him to imagine his oldest daughter in her late 20s or early 30s. I challenged him to think about what she looked like as a woman, where she was living, and what she was doing with her life. He expressed that he hoped she was serving God, had her degree and was pursuing a fulfilling career. I then told him to picture himself sitting at home with her arriving, along with a visitor. This was not just another visitor though. This was the man she was planning to marry, and this was the day she was bringing him home to her father. Then I asked him, "Who is that man?" I remember vividly the bewildered look on my friend's face that day. I told him to go home, put the girls to bed, get a blank piece of paper and a pen, and do this exact mental exercise again. This time, I told him I wanted him to write down who he hoped the man her daughter was bringing home as her future husband would be. I was not talking about height, weight, personal style or eye color. I told him I wanted him to write down what kind of man he was. If he could pick what type of man his daughter would marry in her future, what would he pick? As he left, I told him to come back the next morning. So, he came back bright and early with the paper filled out. It described an amazing man. The characteristics of the man my friend depicted were ones like God-fearing, respectful, faithful, kind, loving, serving, educated, diligent, hard-working, and more. Kind of obvious, right? He then asked me, "Why did you have me do this?" I told him I had no idea how to tell him to do ponytails or where to buy cute girl clothes. I explained I was clueless to some of the daily things he was going to face as a single father. I told him he was simply going to have to trust God, do his best, ask a lot of questions, and probably Google everything else. What I did tell him was that his greatest opportunity was to show his two daughters what an amazing man is. Before he left my office that day, I told him I wanted him to tape that paper on his bathroom mirror so he would see it every day of his life. I read him statistics about how children tend to overwhelmingly follow in their parent's footsteps and even marry people who are similar and exhibit familiar behavioral patterns and characteristics. I explained he would not literally pick his daughter's husband, but in many ways he probably would. The vision written on the paper was not for his daughter; it was for him. As he left, I told my friend, "Now, you go be the man on that paper. If you do, your daughters will know what a Godly man is, and if they don't marry someone accordingly, you will at least know it wasn't

130

because you didn't show it to them." Despite everything he was going through, he now had a clear vision for his future. And to his credit, he has followed it now for years. He is happily remarried. He serves God with a passion. He has overcome depression. He now has a very successful business. His daughters are both working on their degrees. They are kind, sweet, smart and talented. They both serve in church and serve God. About a year ago, my friend told me he still has that paper taped on his bathroom mirror. Write the vision down, God says, make it clear and simple, so they see it can run with it. Never underestimate the power of a vision. It will always inspire you, and others, to run.

What is the vision for your life? I challenge you to get out a piece of paper and start dreaming. Too many are running without direction, or not running at all. In fact, they are walking or even completely stagnated and defeated by life. You do not have to be one of them. You were made to run. You were made to pursue. You were made to dream, conquer, inspire, go places, and do amazing things. You were made to live a great life. Your great life and your fulfilled dreams start with a vision.

131

You Are A Masterpiece!

You Are
A Masterpiece!

How do you view yourself? How do you see yourself as a husband or wife, a father or mother, an employer or employee? What internal perspective do you have that shapes how you view the world around you? I have spent the last few chapters helping to identify issues of the heart that rob us of the peace God has called us to live in and enjoy. Why? Because it is vitally important to have the right foundations within your heart, so the issues of your life are the correct ones. Too often, people view life through negative insecurities picked up as they have grown and matured. Insecurities tend to create a pessimistic and often irrational state of mind. Some common ones are financial, relational and career-related; but, the most prevalent ones are mental and emotional insecurities. It is simple human nature to allow a weakness to formulate into a negative belief, which leads us to make decisions and exhibit behavior accordingly. What is your expectation in life? How do you view your future? Your perspective is your reality, even if your perspective is not the truth; therefore, you cannot allow the wrong self-image to define how you move forward in life. If you do, you will continue to live frustrated, anxious and disappointed. You need to see yourself the way God sees you so you can view your future in the light of God's provision for it. God tells you in 1 Thessalonians 1:3, not only does He love you very much, but He has His hand on your life to do something special. Isn't that spectacular? **God is good. He only does good, and He has good things planned for you and your future.** I cannot emphasize enough that God wants to provide you with an amazing life, not just in Heaven, but also while you are here on the earth. My goal is to simply arm you with logical and Godly tools for you to have a healthy soul, a clean heart and the right mindset. The right mindset for your life and your future is a Godly mindset. To truly gain peace, you must begin to view yourself the way God views you.

In June 2018, my wife Karla and I had the privilege of taking an incredible vacation to Europe. We were celebrating our ten-year wedding anniversary from the year before. An amazing man in our church blessed us with the plane tickets and off we went to Paris, Florence and Rome. I have always been fascinated with history and Karla loves to visit museums to look at art. I have never liked museums. In fact, normally I just endure the art museums with her because I love her and want her to be happy, but it was different in Europe. In Paris, we visited the famed Louvre Museum to see pieces by some of the world's most renowned artists and sculptors like Leonardo da Vinci, Michelangelo, Caravaggio and many others. I marveled at the magnificence of the *Venus de Milo*. We were overwhelmed by the intricate beauty and detail of *Mona Lisa*. In Rome, we visited the Coliseum where the gladiators fought for their lives in the grand spectacles and competitions of ancient times that we have all read about or seen reenacted in cinema. We stood outside of the famed Senate building in the plaza. We walked where Augustus Cesar walked. I got chills as our tour guide showed us the path where historians believe the Apostle Paul was taken to his death. It was a dream come true for me to visit those sites and see those historic locations and buildings. In Florence, we visited the Accademia Gallery. Unlike the Louvre, which holds almost 400,000 works of art and boasts 652,000 square feet, the Accademia Gallery is quite small. In fact, it is said, to truly see and admire every piece of work at the Louvre, you would need to visit every day for three months, but the hotel staff told us we only needed about an hour to see the entire Accademia Gallery. Once inside, you are greeted by a small square room filled to the brim with artwork. From that room, you are led into a long hall that holds the main attraction of this museum. Upon entering this hallway, you are greeted by four unfinished sculptures from Michelangelo called Prisoners. Even unfinished, they are spectacular. But for me, nothing compared to seeing what stood beyond the Prisoners,

The Statue of David. What a work of art! The exquisite beauty, the detail, the size, the stone, the coloring are all perfection. I know my opinion on the matter means very little, but for what it is worth, it is the greatest work of art I have ever laid eyes on. As Karla and I approached it, I remember noticing how quiet it was in the room. In fact, it was almost silent — everyone in awe of Michelangelo's great creation. I quickly realized the concierge was wrong about only needing an hour as Karla and I sat there admiring *The Statue of David* for almost two hours straight. At one point, we actually just sat down to watch other people's reactions to seeing this exquisite sculpture. You simply cannot imagine how amazing it is until you see it. It truly is a masterpiece!

Ephesians 2:10 (NLT) — *"For we are God's masterpiece. He created us anew in Christ Jesus, so we can do the good things He planned for us long ago."*

We see masterpieces all over the earth and throughout our lives. With man, we see priceless works of art, magnificent sculptures, breathtaking buildings and famed monuments. In nature, we see the stars and the sky, the ocean, a color–filled sunset on a summer evening, beautiful rain forests, and much more. Years ago, I sat on a beach in Cancun, Mexico and watched the tide roll in and out in perfect harmony with God's creation, and I was reminded of His creative majesty that designed such a wonderful system of nature. The Bible says you can see God's goodness through His creation, and I agree with that with all my heart. You can even see it in the human body. It is incredible how our skin can regenerate and heal itself after being wounded. It is remarkable how a man and woman can come together in intimacy and create another life while the female body perfectly transforms inside and out to give birth. The human mind alone is simply astonishing; and, to think it was all spoken into existence by an eternal being known as God, our Heavenly Father. So often, we experience God's creation — we see an amazing building like La Sagrada Familia in Barcelona, Spain, or we listen to a musical piece by Mozart — and we say, "That is a masterpiece." And that is exactly what they are. There are masterpieces all throughout the earth created by God and by man. There is no denying their splendor, their ingenuity or their creativity. People travel far and wide to visit them or stand in lines

135

"I am God's masterpiece."

for hours to simply catch a glimpse of one. A Chicago-based hedge fund manager named Kenneth C. Griffin paid $300 million in 2015 for an abstract landscape painting called Interchange by Willem de Kooning. On April 15, 2019, the world watched in horror and grieved as we bore witness to the famed Notre Dame Cathedral de Paris burning for fifteen long hours.

All these masterpieces are incredible, but they are defined as such by man, and they are all temporary. There is one thing and one thing only that God describes as a masterpiece, and that is YOU. **You are God's masterpiece.** Yes, you are. You are God's masterpiece. Wherever you are and however you may feel: man or woman, rich or poor, educated or uneducated, happy or sad. You are a masterpiece! Why don't you just say out loud or to yourself right now? Say, "I am God's masterpiece." Come on, say it again: "I am God's masterpiece." Now, one more time, but this time say it like you actually believe it. Say it with some passion and conviction: "I am God's masterpiece." It feels good to say that, but maybe you do not actually believe it. You might be thinking, "I sure don't feel like a masterpiece — if you only knew, Jared." No, I do not know, and I probably never will. But God knows, and He still calls you His masterpiece. You are not a loser; you are a masterpiece. You are not broken; you are a masterpiece. You are not unworthy; you are a masterpiece. You are not worthless; you are a masterpiece. You have not been forgotten; you are a masterpiece. You are not unloved; you are a masterpiece. You are not an accident; you are a masterpiece. You are not without purpose; you are a masterpiece.

Some time ago, I was walking through Cielo Vista Mall in El Paso. I was by myself on a Tuesday afternoon as my wife had asked me to return an item to a cosmetic store she frequents. You cannot imagine how busy this mall normally is. At one point a few years ago, it was the number one mall in the southwest in terms of daily

136

foot traffic. There are times when you feel like you are just in a swarm of people and can barely navigate freely where you want to go. As busy as it normally is, that was not the case this day. I quickly returned Karla's item and began to head back to my car to go home for the evening. As I walked down the long corridor, I saw a young man who appeared to be around 18 to 20 years old. He had his head down, no expression on his face, and his arms were slumped forward. For some reason, he caught my eye. He looked sad, alone and defeated. As I got closer to him, I was able to read the print on his black, graphic t-shirt. It said, and I quote, "Soy un perdador, I'm a loser baby." I was born in 1979, so early 90s rock is totally my jam. I will never forget hearing Nirvana for the first time. My junior high and high school years were made up of Pearl Jam, Live, Bush, Candlebox, Metallica and all sorts of other similar rock bands. If you are around my age and listened to rock music, you know the phrase on that t-shirt comes from a song by an incredible artist named Beck. As the lyrics go in his most famous song to date, Beck sings repeatedly, "Soy un perdador, I'm a loser baby, so why don't you kill me?" Just so you know, "soy un perdador" is Spanish for "I'm a loser." I grew up listening to this song. I can still sing it on cue, but what a sad set of lyrics. What a terrible way to see yourself and your life. As the young man in the mall walked into a store about twenty steps in front of me, I remember just thinking, "My God, I hope he doesn't actually believe that." To this day, I think about him. I wish I knew who he was. I pray he did not actually feel that way about himself and that it was just a t-shirt.

Please understand, how you see yourself is so important to how you deal with life, and if you are truly going to live the life of peace God declared over you, then you must accept God's identity for you. I know it is hard because you have been told, and maybe even believe, negative things about yourself. You have accepted certain character flaws as permanent scars on your life. Maybe you were lied to about what you are capable of as a person and what to expect in your future. You may have even told yourself that as a humble Christian, there is no way you are allowed to think so positively and confidently. Let me tell you this: it is entirely possible to be humble and believe positively at the same time. In fact, God said you have the right to see yourself the way He sees you; therefore,

137

you have permission to view yourself as the masterpiece that He sees you as. To truly do this though, you must understand what a masterpiece is and how it is created.

The process of becoming a masterpiece:

■ Starts With
1 Your Design

Psalms 139:13-14 (NLT) — *"You made all the delicate, inner parts of my body and knit me together in my mother's womb. Thank you for making me so wonderfully complex! Your workmanship is marvelous—how well I know it."*

I love design. I always have. What I really love is the design process of a building. I have had the privilege of being a part of building two church buildings. Other than the grand opening of the facility, there is nothing more exciting to me then the moment the architect begins to show me the design and the architectural drawings. I am fascinated with looking at renderings and building plans. I find it so interesting to see how an architect can manage space, design efficient ingress and egress, and create beauty while maintaining functionality. I even enjoy combing over electrical and mechanical plans to see what is behind the walls. The design process is what truly determines the finished product. If you do not perfect the design process, you will not build a quality, high functioning facility. In fact, when done right, the design process often takes longer than the actual construction of the building.

The tone of this Psalm is the same as someone standing in view of a great work of art. It is inspired and full of reverence and amazement. *"You made all the delicate, inner parts of my body,"* the Psalmist says. Just like a great architect designs a building from the inside out, so too did God create you. You only view the design of the building from the outside, but you never see what is behind the walls that makes the building actually function. A masterful building is not just what you see, but also what you do not see. God sees you for who you truly are. He sees your worth,

138

your potential and your purpose. In fact, He spent the time to design you exactly the way you are. He looked at every detail. He knows the number of hairs on your head. And that is why He does not believe the lies you have told yourself, and neither should you. His expectation for you has not diminished because of a failed venture or a wrong self-image. Do not discount your Designer, and do not discount what He created.

2 ◼ Continues in Your Creation

Genesis 1:27 (NLT) — *"So God created human beings in His own image. In the image of God He created them; male and female He created them."*

Whose image are you created in? God's image. Notice that He repeats Himself twice in the same verse to tell you that you are created in His image. Just like a parent repeats themselves to their children to emphasize a point, God repeats Himself to us. I believe God knew from the start the world would do everything it can, from the time you are a child all the way until adulthood, to get you to accept the wrong image of yourself. That is why He is redundant. God is making a point that carries great mental and emotional value. He desires for you to see yourself the way He sees you. The sooner you begin to do so, the happier and more confident you will become. It is a great way to live. You are wonderfully complex, designed by the Master Himself with marvelous workmanship designated just for you. Man and woman alike, equally created by the Master Creator Himself. You are wonderful. You are blessed and highly favored of God. You are His child, and He loves you with a great passion and He purposes for you to do amazing things. Please do not allow the devil to convince you otherwise. God's workmanship in you is perfect and created to fulfill His plan for your purpose. The world may write songs that try to convince you that you are a loser, but you are not. You do not have to accept a false identity over your life.

3 Perfected in Christ

Ephesians 2:10 (NLT) — *"For we are God's masterpiece. He created us anew in Christ Jesus, so we can do the good things He planned for us long ago."*

Everything created on earth was designed. Obviously, it was also created. There is something that separates an ordinary creation from an extraordinary one, and that is the perfected execution of the design and creation process. A masterpiece only becomes a masterpiece upon perfection, and quite often, it takes time to perfect. It is said that it took Leonardo da Vinci four full years to perfect the *Mona Lisa*. Historians say he obsessed over every detail. He carried the painting around with him everywhere he went. Every stroke of the brush, every color of the paint, every detail of her face, he had to get right. The building I previously mentioned, La Sagrada Familia, is not yet complete after being worked on for over 500 years now. Michelangelo spent four years painting the Sistine Chapel. Not everything is perfected overnight, and that is okay. You are a work in progress. They key is to allow the work to happen, to make progress, and to grow and mature into completion.

God knew you before you were born. He planned for you to do good things long before you entered your mother's womb. He designed a life for you. He thought of every detail of your incredibly complex human body. God gave you a unique set of passions and skills to empower you into the abundant life He wants you to live. He created you in His perfect image and gave you the amazing gift of Jesus Christ. You are a masterpiece because a piece of the Master Himself lives on the inside of you. At the very moment you allow Jesus to enter your life, your spirit is perfected for eternity. I know on a lot of levels this may challenge your thinking. As you read these statements on being perfected in Jesus, you are reminding yourself you are not perfect. You might even be thinking about the mistake you made last night or how you were rude to someone just a few minutes ago. Obviously, no one is perfect in their flesh in life, but to God, your spirit is what matters. Ultimately, your flesh will wither away, but your spirit will live on for eternity. Your spirit is the real you. Your spirit is the part of you that is divinely connected to your Creator. Your spirit is the most powerful and long-lasting part of your being. When you accept the gift of salvation, the perfection of Jesus enters your spirit and washes away its imperfection. Please know your spirit remains perfect and will do so for eternity even though your flesh and soul still mess up. Over the course of time though, the more you accept who you are in Christ, the more your perfected spirit will begin to overrule and positively affect your imperfect flesh and soul. This is where you will truly see the power of the peace and the grace of God work in your life. You are the person God wants you to be, not because of your imperfect past, but because of His perfect creation. You get to live the life God wants you to live, not because you deserve it, but because He wants you to enjoy it. You can do the great things He planned for you to do, not because of yourself, but because He empowers you to succeed within your purpose.

Your perfection is developed from your spirit through your flesh and soul as you build your life with the right perspective as a masterpiece. You are designed, created and perfected in Jesus Christ. You do not have to try to go be perfect on your own to then come to Him who is perfect. Jesus simply allows us to come to Him and He does the perfecting for us. Jesus even tells us in the Gospels He will come into a person's life and take what is wrong with them and set it right. How incredible is that. Please understand, the enemy does not want you to be empowered to build your life the right way. Jesus wants you to build your life on what is right about Him, and not what is wrong with you. The enemy wants you to build your life on what is wrong with you, and not what is right with God. Two different motives, two drastically different results. The devil would prefer you define your expectation, your decisions and your attitude through your failures, through your insecurities, through your depression, through your regrets and through your mistakes. He will tell you any lie to keep you from understanding who you are in Jesus. Because he knows, in Jesus, the lost are found. In Him, the blind can see. In Him, the sick are healed. In Him, the bound are freed. In Him, the weak are made strong. In Him, the tormented find peace. It is not about you; it is about Jesus and His perfect work inside you. You simply need to start believing the right things about yourself and building your life on what is right about Him and not what is wrong with you.

YOU ARE A MASTERPIECE!

As I mentioned before, I love architecture and design. I enjoy it so much that I have even taken architecture tours when I have visited major cities in the past. I buy housing design magazines. I follow countless design accounts on social media. There is a contemporary style of interior design referred to as minimalistic design. Within this type of design, you will typically find large rooms with clean lines, mostly empty walls and minimal furniture. What is so unique about minimalism is the pricing. One would tend to think that less stuff equals less money. That is usually not at all the case though. In fact, most minimalist buildings and homes come with quite a hefty price tag. Even the small furniture is incredibly expensive. I was flipping through a magazine recently that showcased several mansions in California. One of them was a traditional design and the other was minimalistic. They were the same size and same price. I remember thinking to myself about the minimalistic house, "same price, less stuff." Unfortunately, a lot of people live that way with God. Jesus paid the same price for every person who believes in Him. He paid for you to be forgiven, to be accepted into His family for eternity, and to live a life with a peaceful soul knowing God is providing you with health, welfare, prosperity and every kind of good. His true desire is for His goodness to abound in your life on such a great level that you live with tranquility in your soul due to His favor continuously working on your behalf. He paid the price, but too many live "minimalistic" with him because they will not allow their hearts and minds to be reshaped with the right perspective. Salvation in Jesus is not the end; in fact, it is the beginning. Salvation is the starting point to the amazing life Jesus came to give you. Please do not minimalize the benefits of God for your life by rejecting the gift of perfection He gave you through Jesus. The Bible says that all His promises are yes and amen for you. I hope you will determine to accept nothing less than the entire fulfillment of His promises for your future.

Before we move on, I want to share one of my favorite passages of scripture with you below:

Colossians 1:15-20 (Message) — *"We look at this Son and see the God who cannot be seen. We look at this Son and see God's original purpose in everything created. For everything, absolutely everything, above and below, visible and invisible, rank after rank after rank of angels - everything got started in Him and finds its purpose in Him. He was there before any of it came into existence and holds it all together right up to this moment. And when it comes to the church, He organizes it and holds it together, like a head does a body. He was supreme in the beginning and - leading the resurrection parade - He is supreme in the end. From beginning to end He's there, towering far above everything, everyone. So spacious is He, so roomy, that everything of God finds its proper place in Him without crowding. Not only that, but all the broken and dislocated pieces of the universe - people and things, animals and atoms - get properly fixed and fit together in vibrant harmonies, all because of His death, His blood that poured down from the cross."*

These are incredible words of hope and life spoken to all of us by God. These scriptures reinforce the fact that you have nothing to be ashamed of. You have nothing to be embarrassed about. You have nothing to be insecure about. God created you just the way you are, with a wonderful purpose in mind. He is the Master architect who is designing, creating and perfecting a brilliant set of plans to empower you to build an amazing life. Even when you are hurting, messed up or down, He stands on alert to fix and fit together all the broken and dislocated pieces of your life and work them back into vibrant harmonies. You are a masterpiece. You are God's masterpiece!

143

Not
A Copy

THE MISSING PEACE

Not A Copy

One of the primary characteristics of a masterpiece is that it is always an original. It is never a duplicate or a copy. Copies are just watered-down versions of the original. I have never been to a museum that did not have a gift shop perfectly placed near the exit as I was leaving the facility. Every one of them is filled with mementos, books about the artists, and even replicas of the masterpieces inside the museum. They are nice. They are pretty. You can even buy small versions and mail them home with a personal greeting to your loved ones. But they are not the same as the originals. They do not display the same level of detail, grandeur or magnificence. They usually do not have the same size. They were not paid nearly as much attention to as the original. The handiwork, craftsmanship and uniqueness rarely translate from the original to the copy. They definitely do not carry the same value. You can buy a book of copies for $24.99 or a replica of The Last Supper by Leonardo da Vinci for less than what you pay for a decent steak dinner. The copies serve solely as nice reminders of how exquisite the originals are, but they are not the same.

145

You are not a copy. On December 1, 1913, famed car creator Henry Ford installed the first moving assembly line designed for the mass production of automobiles. Mr. Ford's original invention, the Model T, was a masterpiece of invention at the time. In fact, some would say the assembly line was too. Unlike a vehicle, you were not created on an assembly line. There is no copy of you, and you are not a copy of anyone else. You are not lesser version of your parents or grandparents. Even identical twins have differences. Everyone has their own unique history, life experience and perspective. Nobody sees the world exactly the same. That is one of the true beauties of life. How boring would it be if we were all the same? There would be no ingenuity, creativity, curiosity or progress. Around we would go on the Ferris wheel, bored, stagnated and frustrated. Thank God, we are not copies. God gave you a unique set of ideas, talents and abilities to be used to build the life you want to enjoy.

Originality > Conformism

Galatians 5:25-26 (Message) — *"Since this is the kind of life we have chosen, the life of the Spirit, let us make sure that we do not just hold it as an idea in our heads or a sentiment in our hearts, but work out its implications in every detail of our lives. That means we will not compare ourselves with each other as if one of us were better and another worse. We have far more interesting things to do with our lives. Each of us is an original."*

Romans 12:2 — *"And be not conformed to this world, but be transformed by the renewing of your mind, that you may prove what is that good and acceptable and perfect will of God."*

These scriptures paint a very clear contrast of opposing ways to live your life. In Galatians, we read that God sees us as originals; therefore, we should not live our lives worried or focused on comparing ourselves to those around us. In Romans, we see God does not want us to be conformists. You cannot be both simultaneously. You choose to live as one or the other. You decide to be the original God made you to be, or you live conformed to someone else's plans or the world's ways. It is interesting that the scripture in Galatians tells us not to just hold these truths as an idea in our heads or a sentiment in our hearts. This is important because you can mentally or emotionally assent to the reality that something is the truth without taking hold of it and allowing it to change your life. For example, you can mentally assent to the fact that eating vegetables is healthier for your body than eating French fries without ever changing your habits of eating too many French fries. You can mentally assent to the fact that you should forgive your spouse for a wrongdoing while still holding that wrongdoing against them in your heart. It is easy to recognize truth, it is a whole other challenge to take ownership of that truth to allow it to profoundly affect or influence your behavior. Truth only becomes your truth once you apply it. I urge you right now to choose to allow the truth that you are an original to define how you view your life, and never again conform to the world or its wrongful ways.

Living as an original or as a conformist requires the same amount of effort, but they produce wildly different results. It is the **originals** that change the world. God does not want you to conform to the world, He wants you to transform it; you do that by renewing your mind to His truth. Accept your identity as the masterpiece — the original — that you are. Reject the lies of negativity and insecurity that have held you back. It is the originals that push society forward. The originals reach thousands, open doors, squash challenges, and show the goodness of God working in and through them. Conformists live the way someone else tells them to live. I believe it is the originals that open their hearts and minds to God, allowing Him to lead them to a place of satisfaction, success, promotion and peace. That is why Satan fights to keep you from accepting your true God-given identity. He wants you to conform. He does not want you to set yourself apart from the world. 1 John 2:16-17 in The Message Translation says, *"Don't love the world's ways. Don't love the world's goods. Love of the world squeezes out love for the Father. Practically everything that goes on in the world—wanting your own way, wanting everything for yourself, wanting to appear important—has nothing to do with the Father. It just isolates you from Him. The world and all its wanting, wanting, wanting is on the way out—but whoever does what God wants is set for eternity."* The enemy wants you to fall in love with all the wrong things. He wants to get you to live a life of vanity, possession, greed and lust. He wants you to live ruled by earthly desires. Why? So he can rob you of the call of God on your life. Romans 12:2 told us not to conform so we may prove what is the good and acceptable and perfect will of God. The will of God for you is to live an abundant life of peace, yet too many people chase all the wrong things, and the result is that they are hurting, unfulfilled, lost and broken. The more they pursue, the less happy they are.

147

Do you remember when you had a big dream?

Do you remember the life you wanted to live?

Do you remember the business you wanted to start?

Do you remember when you planned to go back to school and get your master's degree?

Do you remember the marriage you intended to have?

Do you remember when you woke up every day and thought anything could happen, and actually believed it would?

Are you living in those dreams and plans, or have they become a distant memory? If you're not, you can start today. God did not inspire those plans and put those dreams in your heart for you not to see them become a reality. I pray you will no longer allow the world to suck the passion out of you. I pray you will set your affection on God and allow Him to direct your steps to a life well-lived. Be an original and go change the world.

Action > Excuses

Since I was 15 years old, I have exercised routinely five or six days per week. I have always taken physical fitness and healthy living very seriously. I have worked out in many different ways, shapes and forms. I have done classic bodybuilding, taken all sorts of group classes, and even did CrossFit for a few years until I injured my back. At this point in my life, I go to a small gym a friend of mine owns. He gives me daily workouts and helps walk me through them. Despite all my injuries and back surgeries, I'm still in very good shape. The funny thing is, I hate working out. I actually do not enjoy it at all. I love the benefits and the results I get from doing it, but not the hour of hard work and physical exertion. One Monday evening, my trainer started our workout with a 15-minute run on a treadmill. I'm a pretty good runner, but I told him I would much rather go run outside. I hate treadmills. If you are ever convinced that time moves by too fast, go spend five minutes on a treadmill. It's not the running that disagrees with me. In fact, running helps me get a good start to my day. Mostly, I do not enjoy running in place, staring at the calorie counter and distance marker. I would much rather run outside and go somewhere. Running on a treadmill and running outside require the same amount of effort, but at least outside you are going somewhere.

A life lived with action and a life lived with excuses require the same amount of effort, but action takes you somewhere while excuses leave you stuck where you are. Every great vision, every inspired dream, and every creative plan requires action. A vision without a plan of action is just a fantasy. It is a fairy tale that will produce nothing but regret in your life. **You can have results, or you can have excuses, but you cannot have both simultaneously.** Did you know it has been proven that child prodigies are no more successful in life than non-prodigies? That is because talent is not the only key to success. The most successful people in life are the ones who relentlessly pursue what they want to achieve. They do not make excuses. They do not allow challenge, resistance or obstacles to stop them. In fact, excuses are the starting point to conformity, stagnation and failure. Action is the starting point of doing something incredible.

In the Old Testament, Moses had a great dream in his heart. He wanted his people, the nation of Israel, to be freed from captivity to the Egyptians. When Jesus spoke to him to begin pursuing that great dream, Moses had nothing but excuses as his response to the Lord. He said he was not qualified. He said he was not smart enough. He showed his initial lack of trust in God by telling Jesus he did not think the plan would work. He was afraid of failing. He also said he did not have the right skillset and even asked Jesus to send someone else. Nothing but excuse after excuse. The great thing about God is He does not call the qualified; He qualifies the called. You may feel like you are not smart enough, but God has given you the mind of Christ. You may feel like you are not strong enough, but God says when you are weak, His strength is perfected for your weakness. He says if you will ask for wisdom from Him, He will give it to you liberally and without reproach. God tells you to trust Him and He will lead you down an amazing path. Moses made so many excuses that he tried to hand off his dream to a loved one. Ultimately, Jesus' response was to tell Moses to use what was in his hand to get him to what was in his heart. God will always empower you with the knowledge, talents, resources and connections to get you where He has told you to go.

Proverbs 24:3-4 (TLB) — *"Any enterprise is built by wise planning, becomes strong through common sense, and profits wonderfully by keeping abreast of the facts."*

This scripture is a model of how to pursue your passions and build your life.

Wise planning
Common sense
Keeping abreast of the facts

All three of these requirements require action from you. Notice, it does not talk about your history. God did not say your enterprise can only be successfully built if you were raised by a good family. He did not say anything about your educational or financial background. None of that is the key to building your life. Action is the key, not excuses. That means you are going to have to push, strive and pursue opportunity with a determined heart and focused will. You cannot allow challenge and resistance to stop you from moving forward and taking the necessary steps to achieve your goals. You cannot allow limited resources to become the roadblock to your fulfilled dream. You must take initiative, walk with wisdom, trust God and use the talents, abilities and creativity God gives you to get where you want to go.

Taking action to transform your life or your world requires two things. The first is curiosity. How can I make my life better? How can I find peace? Can I be a better spouse? What changes can I make at work to advance our business' objectives? Curiosity simply says, I think there is something better; therefore, it drives creativity and ingenuity. The greatest inventions and scientific discoveries of our time had their roots in simple curiosity. Curiosity itself produces the second requirement: you will have to reject the default. The first thing you do upon purchasing a new smartphone is create your custom configuration. Of course, every iPhone or Android phone comes with factory or default settings. The same is true with you. As you have aged, most likely you have acquired some default settings that have potentially become your excuse to not advance your life. "I just don't have time to exercise." "All the men in my family are this way." "Oh, you know, me and my anxiety." If you are not careful, the negative thought processes produce the wrong identity within your mind and robs you from seeing your full potential. I do not like exercising, but I do it anyway because I refuse to default into an unhealthy lifestyle. Curiosity rejects the default and creates a custom, more desired life.

Being You > Comparison

2 Corinthians 10:12 — *"For we dare not class ourselves or compare ourselves with those who commend themselves. But they, measuring themselves by themselves, and comparing themselves among themselves, are not wise."*

There is a lot of selfishness in this scripture, and that is what comparison is mostly about. A person bound by comparison is 100% focused on themselves and not on the world around them. They are not concerned with honoring God with their lives; instead, they are jealous or envious of someone else's life. The Apostle Paul reveals in this scripture that this is a foolish way to live. Foolishness will never produce anything good for you. The lie of comparison is one of the simplest yet most profound ways the enemy tries to rob you of your originality, your passions and your dreams. It is human nature to compare ourselves to others, particularly if they are more successful than us, but it is no way to live. It keeps your joy and peace bound to others and prevents you from focusing on who God made you to be. You are a completely unique and wonderful person who God created with your own talents, abilities and passions, but you will never maximize any of them if you are constantly focused on what everyone else is doing. In fact, I believe that comparison says to God that what He created in you is not good enough. It says to Him that you do not trust Him, therefore, you are going to attach your life to someone else's plan or vision.

That is exactly what happened to Moses. He told Jesus to send someone else because he had mentally disqualified himself from fulfilling his destiny by comparing his abilities to the people around him. Fortunately, Jesus walked him through his self-doubt, and He will do the same for you.

1 TIMOTHY 4:14

"Do not neglect the gift that is in you."

When I started preaching in 2012 while my mother was fighting for her life against cancer, I was incredibly overwhelmed. My father, Charles Nieman, is a legendary Bible teacher. He is known around the world for his depth of knowledge of the Word of God. He has built one of the top 100 churches in America and travels to preach in some of the most influential ministries in the world today. As he began to give me opportunities to serve on our pulpit at our church, I told myself a lie. I became consumed with trying to preach like he preaches. I even tried to create messages exactly like his. The issue is we have completely different personalities, but I had convinced myself our church would not accept me as their pastor if I was not like my dad. The more I taught, the more frustrated I became. One day, my father walked into my office as I was studying and I said to him, "I just don't know how you do this". We talked for a minute until he said the following words that changed my life in this area: "Stop trying to be me and just go be yourself. The church will love you for who you are and love me for who I am. You will never be me, and that is great." I had set myself on a path of being a copy, a watered-down version of my dad because I was too busy comparing myself to him instead of developing my own gift. Moses told Jesus at the burning bush that he was not talented enough and to send someone else to free the nation of Israel. Jesus' response was to tell Moses to go use what was in his hand to get him to what was in his heart. The Bible says that a man's gift will make a way for him. You are talented and you are gifted. Do not diminish your abilities and never use them because you are unwilling to allow them to develop and mature. In particular, do not neglect the gift God has put on your life by focusing on someone else's gift, or even worse, by being jealous or envious of them. That is such an empty and unfulfilling way to live. It is a complete waste of time and energy. You are not a copy. You are an original. **Comparing what you have with what others have will not bring what they have into your life.** Keep your eyes on your purpose, your calling and your giftings. Go be the absolute best version of the masterpiece God created you to be.

Accountability > Blame

Those are such great catch words? Everywhere you look in society today, you hear people screaming for more accountability and transparency; yet, more and more, blame seems to be taking over. Do we want others to be accountable, but not necessarily ourselves? I believe, and I say this with no judgment whatsoever, blame is becoming the plague of our society today. Everything is everyone else's fault. Blaming others never produces anything good. In fact, blame is the enemy's trap designed to ensnare you and cause you to repeat negative behavior. If you are truly going to transform your life and your world, you must take full ownership of your life and your choices, while allowing God's wisdom to positively influence and guide you.

153

A few years back, I was late to work and I could not find my cell phone. My wife had already left for the day. I searched our bedroom, the closet, the bathroom, the living room and the kitchen. I could just feel my frustration growing as I went back room to room searching over and over again. "What did Karla do with my phone?" I asked myself. "Where did she put it? She's always moving my stuff." My blood was boiling. Oh, the nerve! How dare she! Without thinking, I pulled my phone from my back pocket and, with my mind in auto pilot, I dialed her. Yes, that is right. I was calling my wife with my "lost" phone, still angry with her for putting my phone somewhere it shouldn't be. As she answered, I realized I was on my phone. It was not my brightest moment, but that is what blame does. It is amazing how easy it is to just blame others. It is almost human nature. It causes you to project your issues onto someone or something else, when the first place you should look is at yourself.

Accountability always moves your life forward. It produces progress. It allows for wisdom and counsel to be spoken and received as you navigate the opportunities and challenges you face. Accountability produces improvement, which obviously produces better results. Better results produce more joy, satisfaction and fulfillment. Fulfillment produces peace. Accountability seeks solutions and pursues the truth. Blame seeks to find fault and often denies the truth. Job 5:6 in the Message Translation says, *"Don't blame fate when things go wrong; trouble doesn't come from nowhere."* Deciding who is to blame should not be the focus of your life when things are not working out the way you intended. The first place you should look is at yourself, while opening your heart up to the grace of God. The most successful people in life, the originals who change the world, hold themselves to the highest standards of responsibility and accountability.

Who is at fault should not be the issue of your life. "What can I do better?" That is the question you must constantly ask yourself. If you allow your life to be controlled by other people's actions, you will have plenty of blame to hand out, but you will also never fulfill your destiny. Blame only perpetuates a victim mentality, and that is exactly what Satan wants. He wants you to be victimized into defeat and despair. But you are not a victim, you are a victor. You are a conqueror. You are mighty in God. It is time to fight back, make the changes you need to make, determine to overcome, and be the original God created you to be. Go transform your world.

On Purpose, For A Purpose

On Purpose,
For A Purpose

As a pastor, I spend significant amounts of time talking to people, praying with them, answering questions and giving counsel based on various situations people find themselves in. Quite often, they start coming to church and developing a relationship with God. While doing so, much of their thinking and identity begins to be challenged, in a good way, by what they are hearing and reading in God's Word. The questions I hear the most from many of those conversations are, "What is my calling? What is my purpose?" People want and need to know why they are here on this earth. The questions they ask are questions we have all asked ourselves at some point, if not repeatedly, in our lives. The issue is people do not always find the answers; therefore, they feel like they are just existing. If this becomes a reality, a sense of uselessness and fatalism begins to grow. You were not created by the Almighty God of this universe to simply work, pay taxes and die. Life is so much more than that. You are not here by chance. You are not here by accident. The Bible says God desired to create mankind and He delights in having a relationship with us. He sent Jesus to die on the cross for your sins to be forgiven so you can spend eternity in Heaven with Him. You were designed, created and perfected as an original masterpiece by God — on purpose, for a purpose. I hope you never lose sight of that. Knowing what you are called to do and having a sense of purpose adds such importance, value and clarity to who you are and what you do in life. That understanding produces direction, inspires determination, and empowers discipline and consistency. Having a clear sense of what your purpose is will be a continual driving force toward fulfillment and satisfaction.

God's plan and purpose for your life is perfect, and it will be fulfilled if you open your heart and mind to it. His purpose is to lead you from the abundant life of peace, joy and happiness here on earth to the eternal life in Heaven. As perfect as His purpose is though, we are not. We are greatly influenced by society, fear, doubts and insecurities. The beauty is God is greater than those negative influences, and all of them can be overcome and rooted out of your soul by accepting who God made you to be and growing in your relationship with Jesus and His Word. In fact, the greatest decision you can make in your life is to incline your ear to the wisdom of God and follow His path for your life. The book of Proverbs teaches that wisdom is far more valuable than any earthly possession, including gold and silver. You simply cannot underestimate the value of trusting in God's way of living. A life lived in reverence to the Lord is a well-formed life, existing in seasons of confidence, integrity, favor and fulfillment. In fact, Proverbs 3:24 shows the direct, peace-based results that arise from trusting in God's plan: *"When you lie down, you will not be afraid; yes, you will lie down and your sleep will be sweet."* As you grow in God, you become more emboldened to accomplish His will for your life. The more you accomplish, the more He produces good on your behalf. The more good He produces, the more you are filled with satisfaction and happiness. When you walk in God's purpose, you walk securely. When you walk in God's purpose, you walk confidently. When you walk in God's purpose, you walk with peace.

158

Ephesians 2:10 (NLT) — *"For we are God's masterpiece. He has created us anew in Christ Jesus, so we can do the good things He planned for us long ago."*

This scripture reveals that God created His masterpiece, you, to do good things. That has been and will always be His purpose for your creation. The night the angel of God declared peace on earth toward all men, He declared good. God does good things for us, so we can do good things in our lives. And, let me be clear, you can do the good things He planned for you. You can do ALL things through Christ who strengthens you. That is one commonality all Christians have. Ephesians 5:1 tells us to be imitators of God. We are to reproduce in our lives what God has done for us. His goodness is meant to shine on you and through you. You are blessed by

God to be a blessing. God wants you to enjoy His blessing, but He always intends for you to pass it along to the world around you. His blessing on your life should speak of His goodness, grace and mercy abounding toward you in everything you do. Your life is meant to be a living representation of His glory and provision all around you. But sometimes, people get so busy in life or so discouraged by disappointment that they lose sight of their purpose. Life can be incredibly demanding. You can get caught in a mundane routine and fail to realize God has a greater purpose in what you are doing and where you are going. God gave you hopes and dreams so you **can do them**, not for you to be frustrated by them.

2 Timothy 1:9 — *"Who has saved us and called us with a holy calling, not according to our works, but according to His own purpose and grace which was given to us in Christ Jesus before time began."*

This is a fantastic and encouraging scripture that helps every Christian to understand God has not only saved them, but He has also called them and given their life a great purpose. Before we go any further, please understand that every person who serves God has a calling and a purpose, and purpose cannot be undone. Once God directs the plan for your life, no one can usurp His plan. In fact, this scripture says your calling is not based on your works, but rather, on His purpose. This reality vividly highlights the beauty of the grace of God. One of the Bible definitions of God's grace is His divine favor and empowerment bestowed upon you. God empowers you to succeed within the calling and purpose He has designed for your life. It is His grace that allows you to maximize your life in Him and accomplish all He has planned for you.

159

You have been saved and called. Salvation is not the end. It is the beginning of a called life. Salvation is the starting point to walking down a Godly path that leads you to the abundant life Jesus wants you to enjoy. I do not want to just be saved. I do not want to float through life aimlessly. I do not want to live empty and devoid of fulfillment. I do desire to know where I am going, what I am doing, and why I am doing it. I want to live called with an amazing purpose. I hope you feel the same way. When you understand what your calling is, you can begin to live totally focused with complete intention to do everything you can to see your calling fulfilled.

Let's begin to answer the questions I asked at the beginning of the chapter:

What is Your Calling?

Romans 12:4-6 — *"For as we have many members in one body, but all the members do not have the same function, so we, being many, are one body in Christ, and individually members of one another. Having then gifts differing according to the grace that is given to us, let us use them: if prophecy, let us prophesy in proportion to our faith."*

As I discussed in the previous chapter, your life is completely and wonderfully unique. The same is true for your calling. Everyone's calling is different. We are all part of the body of Christ, but no two of us serve the same function. Thank God! Not much would get done if we all did the same thing. There would be no creativity and progress if everyone thought the same way and presented identical ideas and solutions. We need differing perspective and points of view to challenge the status quo. The truth is, we even need conflict — healthy and respectful conflict, of course. We need diversity in life. We need it in our families, in our businesses, in our schools and our churches. Your calling is defined by your God-given dreams, passions, talents and desires. Your calling can even vary across the different roles you play in life. For example, I have a calling as a father that differs from my calling as a friend. My calling as a husband differs from my calling as a pastor. Every one of us serves in differing roles and functions in the vast space that defines our lives; therefore, your calling is adjusted within each of those roles to fulfill the necessary functions. Notice that the above scripture says, *"having gifts differing according to the grace that is given to us, let us use them."* Your gifts are a part of your calling. It is your gifts that God will anoint and use to empower your life into success, welfare, prosperity and all kinds of good. The Bible says a man's gift will make a way for him. I have a gift to speak the Word of God publicly. I do not have a gift to sing and lead worship. I must use the gift God gave me to fulfill my calling as a pastor at our church while also allowing the amazing musicians and worship leaders to use their gifts accordingly. If we tried to mix or exchange our callings, we would all wind up frustrated, stressed and angry with ourselves and each other. The people around us would wind up feeling the same way too.

What are you good at? What comes naturally to you? What do you enjoy doing? What activity brings you satisfaction and fulfillment? Your calling can be found in your answers to those questions. The key is to start using your calling. The danger is to ignore it or even reject it. 1 Timothy 4:14 tells us not to neglect the gift that is within us. You will never live the life you want to live if you are focused on what you do not have rather than being focused on what you do have. Too often though, people tend to not value their giftings at the highest level, and as a result those giftings are never fully developed. If God gave you a skill, a talent or a resource, your responsibility is to watch over it, invest in it, develop it and maximize it to its fullest extent. There is something so great, and refreshing, when you allow yourself to become comfortable with who God made you to be and you move forward within your calling. That is the only path that leads to a peace-filled life. Neglect will get you nowhere good. You should constantly endeavor to improve, to work hard, to get smarter, to adjust and to strive for greatness. The best thing you can do right now is pursue the passions within your heart with your might, while trusting God has and will give you the resources to achieve them. It may take a while, but finish what you started. Do not give up. It may be hard, but nothing amazing in life comes without challenge. Success is difficult, but it is also worth it.

2 Corinthians 10:13 — *"We, however, will not boast beyond measure, but within the limits of the sphere which God appointed us—a sphere which especially includes you."*

You have your own uniquely created and appointed sphere that your life functions within. The key to a fulfilled calling is to live within that sphere of influence and ability. Human nature will respond to this scripture by saying that it is restrictive and limiting, but human nature is wrong in this instance. Living within your sphere, your calling, gives your life direction. In fact, it allows you to function with complete clarity in your decision making. Having some boundaries on your life allows to you stay focused on the right things while not being distracted by the wrong things. We do this at our church all the time. We are known for great worship, faith-filled prayer and a wide-ranging community initiative, but we are mostly known for teaching the Word of God in a clear and concise way. We do it in a manner that allows people from all walks of life to grasp hold of it in a relevant and useful way so they can apply it in their everyday lives.

I have a lot of friends in the ministry and I visit churches around the world constantly. I am always amazed by the varying callings God has placed on them. Many of them are thriving in certain aspects of ministry that God has never called our church to do. My response is not jealousy or frustration; rather, I try to be inspired and excited by what they are accomplishing through the grace of God. The beauty of it is there is no wrong in this. We are all simply staying within the sphere God placed us in. The key to fulfilling your calling is to not neglect it, and the Bible shows us exactly how not to do that very thing.

2 Corinthians 10:12 — *"For we dare not class ourselves or compare ourselves with those who commend themselves. But they, measuring themselves by themselves, and comparing themselves among themselves, are not wise."*

2 Corinthians 10:14 — *"For we are not overextending ourselves (as though our authority did not extend to you), for it was to you that we came with the gospel of Christ."*

These two scriptures identify five clear ways you neglect the call of God on your life.

▬ Do Not
1 Class Ourselves

Attempting to identify yourself with a specific or isolated class is incredibly selfish. In fact, every practice highlighted in the above scriptures is selfish, and the Apostle Paul tells us living this way is foolish and not wise. Classing yourself implies a sense of entitlement. The idea that you are of a higher or lower class than others implies you either deserve or do not deserve certain opportunities or giftings. The grace of God, however, is a gift of God's undeserved favor on your life. The kingdom of God is not a class-based kingdom. The kingdom of God is a grace-based kingdom. You do not get the life you deserve; you get the life God wants you to have. Classing yourself above others tends to lead to arrogance, pride, haughtiness, and other unattractive and ungodly characteristics. Jesus made very clear to us in the gospels that if we will be faithful over what He gave us, He will make us rulers over much. It is God who we live to represent because it is God who promotes us. Conversely, classing yourself lower than others implies you are not good enough or deserving of the life God gave you, which could disqualify you from your calling. That is an insecurity you must confront. God does not call the qualified; He qualifies the called. Jesus qualifies you, whether you feel you deserve it or not. The goodness of God is provided because of who He is, not who you are. Your part to play in this transaction is to simply receive His goodness, accept your calling, and begin using it for the glory of God.

■ Do Not
2 Compare Ourselves

It is important to note that once again God's Word highlights the dangers of living with comparison in your heart. Comparison is such a fruitless road to walk down in your life. It will never produce a personally fulfilled calling; rather, it will produce only a sense of emptiness and longing. Neither of these emotions lead to peace. I vividly remember a conversation with my father when I was about 12 years old. He had just picked me up from school, and I proceeded to tell him how frustrated I was that I was not the best basketball player in my sixth-grade class at Faith Christian Academy. I was feeling down about myself. In my mind, the obviously unwarranted dream of heading straight to the NBA after high school was slipping away. There was one kid in my class who was far superior to me, and I remember being solely focused on how good he was compared to me. My dad listened and calmly responded with the following words: "There will always be someone bigger, faster, stronger or smarter than you. Never give energy to what God gave someone else. You focus on what He gave you." Those are wise words for all of us to live by. God made you exactly the way He wanted you to be and He will give you the desires of your heart. He does not promise to give you the desires of someone else's heart. Focus on who God made you to be so He can help you fulfill your dreams.

▬ Do Not
3 Commend Ourselves

Have you ever met a person who always has to outdo everyone, no matter what is being discussed? I call them the one-upper. They are full of stories, often exaggerated, highlighting and boasting about their exploits and accomplishments. This type of behavior is typically displayed in an attempt to prop themselves up in other people's minds while debasing those same people. What these people fail to realize is they aren't proving anything, nor are they nearly as impressive as they think they are. Great accomplishments speak for themselves and do not need to be bragged about. It is such a selfish way to behave. I believe it is born out of pride and arrogance. It is the antithesis of humility. If you know anything about the words of Jesus, you know He directed us to live with humility. In fact, in Matthew 23:12, He said, *"And whoever exalts themselves will be humbled, and he who humbles himself will be exalted."* When you stay within your sphere and your calling, the results of the goodness of God manifesting in your life will say plenty about who you are, what you believe, and what you are doing. They will speak for themselves. You will have nothing to prove because God will do it for you. Jesus said you will know a person by the fruit their life bears.

▬ Do Not
4 Measure Ourselves

You are going to find life very challenging and frustrating if you are constantly measuring yourself against others. If that is the focus of your mind, you will either never measure up or you will measure others down. If you are always trying to measure up, you will live with a sense of not being good enough or a feeling of inadequacy. Obviously, that is not a peaceful or confident way to go about your life. On the flip side of that is living as if people are beneath you. I've had people treat me like that, as I'm sure you have, and it is not a nice experience. There is nothing about Godliness that implies that we should demean or degrade people around us. In fact, we are told by Jesus to love and serve them, not judge and humiliate them. Both characteristics are born out of insecurities. Always trying to measure up to others is a "not good enough" insecurity. Demeaning or degrading others is a "too good for others" insecurity. Both are inappropriate and need to be addressed. It is not our job to measure or judge others; it is our job to love them and use our calling for good.

■ Do Not
5 Overextend Ourselves

It is important to note that overextending yourself is the only one of the five ways to neglect your calling that is not an emotion or a state of mind; however, it will lead to negative emotions. Nowadays, it is so easy to get overextended. You can work too much. You can stress while attempting to please everyone. You can overcommit your time to work, hobbies and family activities. You can worry about the wrong things. During the COVID-19 pandemic of 2020 I learned a great personal lesson about stress and worry. That lesson was to not allow myself to be burdened by things I could not control. As I am sure you recall, each state and our country changed almost weekly due to stay-at-home orders, business shutdowns, curfews and more. At the beginning of it all, I was so upset, anxious and stressed over each decision being made. Finally, I woke up one morning and said to myself, "What's the use?" My being upset was not changing the decisions. My losing sleep was not the concern of our government leaders. The only person being negatively affected by it was me. In truth, I had plenty to focus my energy on, and things I had no control over needed to not stay on my list. The world's cliché for what I am talking about is to "major on the majors and minor on the minors." Developing and maintaining the proper boundaries and limits on your life is critically important to establishing a long-term path of physical, mental and emotional health. If you continuously feel overburdened or burnt out, you need to immediately reevaluate the priorities of your time, focus and effort. The danger is to be overextended in a lot of areas, while not affording the right area (your calling) the proper attention to develop and produce the fulfillment and satisfaction it is intended to produce.

What is Your Purpose?

Now that you have an understanding about what your calling in life is, it is important to also discover your purpose. Every person deserves to know and understand the reason they exist. Knowing your purpose can be a strong driving force in your life. It gives you reason to wake up in the morning, to strive to do amazing things and to never stagnate. I believe purpose propels your life beyond the immediate and into the long-term. Purpose influences the overall theme and direction of your life. It is infinite, more than finite. Living to honor your purpose is quite possibly the most important decision you can make for your life and your future. It is 100% worth your time to understand why you are here so you can passionately pursue it in everything you do.

Let's first understand that purpose and success are not directly connected. You can have plenty of success without knowing your purpose. I have spent countless hours with people who are incredibly successful in business and finance, but they are miserable in spirit. **Success does not equal significance.** Significance brings fulfillment, meaning and value, and that is exactly what knowing your purpose will add to your life.

Philippians 2:13 (NIV) — *"For it is God who works in you to will and to act in order to fulfill His good purpose."*

As wonderfully unique and individual your calling is for your life, your purpose is not. In fact, as Christians, God has designed our purpose for us. We all have the same purpose, and with God's help, it will come to pass. The realization of the purpose, though, has a lot do with your decision making. You simply choose to accept God's purpose for your life and move forward to fulfill it, or you do not. The purpose of God should be at the forefront of your mind and set as a priority within your household and your planning. Functioning within this amazing purpose should heavily influence where you live, what you do, and how you do it. This takes discipline and discretion to allow the wisdom of God to lead your life, so you can avoid making decisions that negatively affect your God-given destiny. A beautiful truth of the goodness of God is He will work through even the worst circumstances and decisions. Your bad choices or behavior are not greater than His power to restore and bring recovery into your situation. Romans 8:28 (NIV) says, *"And we know that in all things God works for the good of those who love Him, who have been called according to His purpose."* At the very moment you point your affection toward God, His goodwill will be working to fulfill favor, blessing and wisdom in your life for you to walk in your purpose.

Matthew 5:13-16 — *"You are the salt of the earth; but if the salt loses its flavor, how shall it be seasoned? It is then good for nothing but to be thrown out and trampled underfoot by men. You are the light of the world. A city that is set on a hill cannot be hidden. Nor do they light a lamp and put it under a basket, but on a lampstand, and it gives light to all who are in the house. Let your light so shine before men, that they may see your good works and glorify your Father in Heaven."*

167

These words that Jesus spoke make it very clear how we are to live our lives: we are to be the salt of the earth and the light of the world. Regardless of your calling, your role, where you live or what you do, **you are to be salt and light.** That is the God-given purpose to every Christian on this planet. We all have different histories, we all think uniquely, and we are completely original in our design as His masterpieces; but, our purpose is the same. This is why we are here, and this is what we are supposed to accomplish. Being the salt of the earth and the light of the world should motivate and drive our choices, words and actions in our houses, at work and in our communities. Letting your light shine before others so they may see your good works and glorify God must be the motivation behind every decision we make, every action we take, and every interaction we engage in. There is no purpose on earth greater than bringing God glory through your life. Consequently, there is no satisfaction more fulfilling than knowing you played a part in positively affecting someone else's life and potentially introducing them to the unconditional love and divine peace of God.

To be the salt of the earth literally means the following: We as the children of God are to circulate among the people of the earth, and by our doctrine and our example, we are to influence them. What a great definition. Being a Christian with a great purpose is not complicated. You and I both exist to go into the world and show people the love and the goodness of God. Notice the definition says, "by our doctrine and our example." Isn't that so important? I think we can all agree, words without corresponding action are basically worthless. You can say whatever you want, but if your actions contradict your words, trust will be lost and your words will mean little to nothing. Our doctrine as Christians will only take our influence as far as our actions line up with them. You are called by God to go into the world, not to hide from it, and influence it in a positive manner for the glory of God. Jesus also said salt becomes useless when it loses its flavor. Well, of course it does. I looked that phrase up in a Bible concordance and it means we lose sight of our purpose. Never let go of the fact that God has purposed you to be in the world and not of the world. You, in whatever your calling is, function to change the world, and that is exactly why the world pressures Christians of all walks of life to compromise, to get worn down, and to ultimately be quiet about God and His peace abounding in your life. The world wants you to forget your purpose. The enemy wants the world to negatively influence you into a life of sin, compromise, anxiety, depression and unfulfillment. Much of the way he accomplishes this in your life is by causing you to forget you are the salt of the earth. You are here to make a difference. Your life can be a beacon of hope and good to those around you. You do not have to give in to the world and its way. On the contrary: you can change the world!

You are also the light of the world. I just love the imagery of that statement. I am inspired by that fact that Jesus says I carry His light, and I can take that light into a dark world. Darkness cannot put light out. Light puts out darkness. The word light in the literal text of the Bible means to be a dispenser of moral goodness. This world you live in needs light. It needs you to let your light shine. The world needs millions of Christians to go out and do good. Not just say good things, but follow up our good words with good action. We need to love with all our hearts. We need to have compassion for people who are hurting. We need to feed the hungry and clothe the naked. We need to weep when others weep and rejoice when others rejoice. We need to stand for what is right and stand against what is wrong. We need Christians who are far more loving and accepting of people than we are judgmental and condemning. The light of Jesus shines throughout the world through our good works, not just our words. The world around us should be able to identify the goodness of God in our lives without us having to even say anything. They may not be able to articulate it, but they should know there is something that sets us apart from them. It is not enough to say I love Jesus if there is no evidence of that love in my life. Truly, it is the goodness of God that leads people to change and to repentance. It is our job as Christians to show His goodness.

James 2:17 — *"Thus also faith by itself, if it does not have works, is dead."*

This is a powerful and challenging scripture that complements the meaning of being the light of the world. Faith without works, or corresponding action, is dead. One translation says faith without benevolent action is a mockery. Claiming faith to the world is not sufficient. Genuine faith produces good works. In a lot of ways, this is where Christianity has gone wrong. For too long, many Christians have stood on the sidelines of the game of life and pointed out the problems of the world without getting in the game to help provide solutions. We are to be like Jesus. Jesus never pointed out a problem without providing the solution. Profession of faith does not mean possession of faith. Your faith is given to you to be useful, to produce good, and to lead to a positive impact in your life and others. That truth should drive you in everything you do. If we want society to change, it starts with us. If you want your family to serve God, it starts with you. You are the salt of the earth and the light of the world. Your purpose is to make a difference in the world around you for the glory of God.

1 Timothy 6:17–19 (NIV) — *"Command those who are rich in this present world not to be arrogant nor to put their hope in wealth, which is so uncertain, but to put their hope in God, who richly provides us with everything for our enjoyment. Command them to do good, to be rich in good deeds, and to be generous and willing to share. In this way they will lay up treasure for themselves as a firm foundation for the coming age, so that they may take hold of the life that is truly life."*

Society would have you believe that a good life is a rich life filled with countless material possessions. It would have you put your hope in acquiring status and acceptance in certain clubs or social circles. The world wants you to believe happiness is found in a car, house, vacation, drink or drug. The world is a liar. None of those things produce inner fulfillment and sustained gratification. Are nice things great? Of course, they are. The problem is not wanting a nicer house or a promotion. We all want that, and there is nothing wrong with having that desire. The problem is not expecting peace to arrive from those things alone. True fulfillment is found in doing good, being rich in good deeds, and living a generous life. You are here on purpose. You are here for this purpose! You are here to do good!

Cherished, Valued, Loved

Cherished, Valued, Loved

As I mentioned previously, my wife and I had the privilege of visiting the famed Louvre Museum in Paris, France a few years ago. As you know, millions travel from all over the world to see incredible, historical and priceless works of art and statues on display there at the former castle-turned-museum. The most infamous work of art there is *The Mona Lisa*. I will never forget what it was like to find and view her. It is a completely different experience to see her than any other masterpiece in the facility. The security measures taken to protect this painting are incredible. Unlike the rest of the pieces, you cannot just walk up to *The Mona Lisa* and admire Leonardo da Vinci's greatest work. To begin with, the small (2', 6" x 1', 9") frame is guarded by multiple glass enclosures. You can only get within about 20 feet of the painting. There are layers of ropes and numerous security guards standing guard to keep anyone from getting too close. I witnessed one guard forcibly remove a person who attempted to cross the rope barrier. Of course, the ropes are in addition to the multimillion-dollar security camera system also in place, but out of sight to the public. The measures are incredible, but also necessary and completely understandable. Of course, this once in a lifetime masterpiece is guarded, protected and watched over to ensure its safe keeping. *The Mona Lisa* is one of the most cherished and loved works of art ever created, so we would expect nothing less regarding its security and protection.

The last three chapters of this book have all been focused on the central theme that you are God's masterpiece. I have been intentional about spending time on this topic because you must have the right mindset about who you are, what you are doing, and why you are here. You will never truly experience the peace of God within your heart and mind if you do not view yourself correctly. Knowing your self-worth is critical to having a healthy soul. I believe every masterpiece has four things in common: every masterpiece is designed, created and perfected over time. They are originals, created on purpose for a purpose. They are cherished, valued and loved. God sees you as a masterpiece, and I hope you are beginning to see yourself the way God sees you. Every masterpiece has great value, and so do you. People pay massive amounts of money for pieces of art, flawless diamonds, incredible mansions, historic relics, centuries-old sculptures and more. We will travel far and wide, stand in lines for hours, and pay entrance fees at museums just to catch a glimpse of a masterpiece. Those same museums will spend millions of dollars annually to protect, guard and secure these treasured items and works of art we so dearly love. That is exactly what God does for you and your life. He is your refuge and your fortress. He is your shield and your buckler. The Bible says He watches over you to take care of and guard you. One of the names of Jesus is Jehovah Nissi — meaning He is your banner of protection. He watches over you, guards you and protects you, and because you are His masterpiece, He loves you at a level unmatched by anyone or anything in this universe. Everything good God has done, is doing, or ever will do for humanity comes from His unconditional love for us.

John 3:16-17 — *"For God so loved the world that He gave His only begotten Son, that whoever believes in Him should not perish but have everlasting life. For God did not send His Son into the world to condemn the world, but that the world through Him might be saved."*

Quite often, as we view a masterpiece, we will utter the phrase, "that's priceless." The value is beyond measure. In fact, these items are usually held at such regard that no one would ever allow them to be put up for sale in the first place. It would take an enormous price for such a masterpiece to switch hands from one owner to another. You are priceless to God. That is how much value He placed on humanity. He loves you so much that He sent His Son to die for you to have the opportunity to be in relationship with Him, now and for eternity. He cherishes you at such an immense level that Jesus

CHAPTER 15

suffered, became sin, and was made a curse so you and I can be forgiven, loved and blessed all the days of our lives. God is good and He only does good for you because He values you so much.

1 Corinthians 13:13 says, *"And now abide faith, hope, love, these three; but the greatest of these is love."* Truly, the love of God is the greatest gift ever given to mankind. It is the greatest gift because it is the eternal gift. When you are in Heaven, you will not need faith anymore. When you are in Heaven, you will also not need hope anymore. Conversely, when you are in Heaven, you will still need love for it is truly the love of God that will keep you in relationship with Him for eternity, and nothing can disconnect you from it. Too many people have been taught for years and years that God's love is conditional and dependent on your behavior. This could not be further from the truth. God is love. God is only love, and you cannot separate God from His love. It knows no limits, and it never runs out. That is your reality as a child of God. You are loved relentlessly and unconditionally by the God of the Heavenlies, and there is nothing anyone can do to change it. The Apostle Paul wrote in Romans 8 that not even the worst sins listed in scripture can separate you from God's love. There is simply nothing you can do to cause God not to love you wholly and completely.

175

It is a travesty when God is described to people as anything other than love. People by the millions have been taught God is angry. Religion has implied God will punish people depending on their behavior. I have heard it said that God is despondent about the suffering of Jesus for our sins and is therefore actively seeking revenge on humanity. People say, "God's going to get you for that... God will be disappointed in you... God did that to you to teach you a lesson... God is going to smite you..." Obviously, none of these statements are true because none of these statements are describing anything related to the characteristics of love. God's love is not determined by how good you were last week, or whether you deserve it or not. If it was, none of us would qualify to be loved by Him. We would all eventually fall out of His graces, but that is not going to happen. The love of God is not determined by human function or behavior, it is determined by His nature. I repeat, God is love, and you cannot separate Him from Who He is.

The shame of the misperception of God is that it robs people of truly enjoying their relationship with Him and having the correct expectation for their life with Him on their side.

Here is what the Bible (1 Corinthians 13:4–8) says love is and does:

Love suffers long.
Love is kind.
Love does not envy.
Love does not parade itself.
Love is not puffed up.
Love does not behave rudely.
Love does not seek its own.
Love is not provoked.
Love thinks no evil.
Love does not rejoice in iniquity.
Love rejoices in the truth.
Love bears all things.
Love believes all things.
Love hopes all things.
Love endures all things.
Love never fails!

This is who God is. This the character and attitude of God. This is the sentiment God has for you. God is not angry with you. He is not judging nor trying to do bad things to you. God has not left you. You cannot exhaust the love of God, nor wear it out nor overburden the love of God with your issues. You are His masterpiece, and he cherishes every aspect and detail of your existence. He values you at such an extreme level He will do anything to protect and provide for you. He is for you and not against you. God will never fail you because God is love and love never fails. You fail, but God does not, and that is something you need to carry with you always. We all have sinned and fallen short of the glory and goodness of God, but God loves us so much that He does not pull it from us in our failure. The challenge then becomes to not judge yourself, punish yourself, and separate yourself from God's love because of your mistakes or sin. That is one of the most difficult areas to overcome within your mind. It is almost human nature. We do wrong so we believe we should be punished. We mess up so we believe we are a mess-up.

He loves you more than He hates your sin.

Those of you who have kids understand this concept very well. You do not stop loving your children when they make a mistake. You teach them, show them what is right, and move forward. Your love, your hand of protection, and your grace upon your children exists because they are your children, not because they are perfect or have done no wrong. In fact, you love them knowing they are far from perfect, but you love them anyway. The enemy will always try to use your imperfection as a tool to bring self-judgment and condemnation into your life. If you allow it to happen, eventually you will stop praying, worshipping and going to church. You will grow far from God and feel like you are alone. The lie you will tell yourself in judgment is you must get yourself right before you can go to God. The truth is Jesus says to come to the One who is right, and He will make you right! Isn't that incredible? The goal of the enemy is to separate you from the love of God, therefore, separating you from His peace. The beautiful truth is God accepts you just the way you are and loves you enough to help you not stay that way. You are a masterpiece that God bought with the blood of Jesus on the cross. He paid the ultimate price for you, and He paid it in full. Jesus came to save the world, not to judge or condemn it. If Jesus is not judging you or condemning you, it is about time you to stop judging or condemning yourself.

177

Romans 5:3-5 (Message) — *"There's more to come: We continue to shout our praise even when we're hemmed in with troubles, because we know how troubles can develop passionate patience in us, and how that patience in turn forges the tempered steel of virtue, keeping us alert for whatever God will do next. In alert expectancy such as this, we're never left feeling shortchanged. Quite the contrary—we can't round up enough containers to hold everything God generously pours into our lives through the Holy Spirit!"*

This scripture is powerful because it counters what our human tendency is when we make mistakes, don't feel right about ourselves, are going through difficult seasons or even when we sin. By nature, you most likely punish yourself mentally or emotionally for your mistake. If you are like me, you feel like you cannot go to God in prayer or worship. At a minimum, you probably feel like you somehow negatively affected God's intention toward you. That could not be further from the truth.

The Apostle Paul instructs you to continue to praise God even during times of trouble. The reality of God is His love is more powerful than your sin. **He loves you more than He hates your sin.** You cannot out sin God's grace. Now, that is not a license to sin; in fact, it should produce gratitude within your heart and mind toward God for His goodness. Even when you feel like anything but a masterpiece, God is commending His love and peace toward your life because a piece of Him lives within you. What an amazing truth this is as you go forward on this journey of peace. Never again be tormented by your mistakes, your shortcomings, your misgivings or your failures. Do not isolate in those moments, disappear from your church, stop praying and worshipping God. Do not stop connecting with the Godly people in your life. The key here is to go to God while simultaneously making the changes you know you need to make so as to not repeat the negative behavior. Even in your worst moment, this scripture shows God is still pouring out His generosity into your life. And, there is more to come! You just cannot contain how great God's love is for you. I think it is actually something humanity cannot fully grasp. Because our love is conditional, we struggle to understand and accept God's unconditional love. Here is the great news: you do not have to understand something for it to be true.

God's Word goes on to show us that the love of God results in great inner strength and resolve arising from the purity of the forgiveness

178

you receive from Him. There is nothing that can change how God feels about you. God's mood toward you never wavers. He is not fickle like you and me. His love is not determined by whether or not He slept well or if He woke up on the right side of the bed. His love is not going to be negatively affected by who is President of the United States or what political party is in control of Congress.

Be careful to never try to humanize God. He is not us and He is not like us. Our love is conditional. His is not. That is why His love is perfect and never fails. The expanse of God and His effort to reach His masterpieces is something of complete greatness and majesty. You are worth everything to God. Just like humans go to extreme lengths to see earthly masterpieces, God will do anything to be in relationship with you. He wants you to experience His divine love, plumb the depths of it, experience the breadth of it and test its lengths. Truly, it is the love of God that sent us Jesus to allow Him to declare peace on earth and goodwill toward men.

Romans 8:31-39 (Message) — *"So, what do you think? With God on our side like this, how can we lose? If God didn't hesitate to put everything on the line for us, embracing our condition and exposing Himself to the worst by sending his own Son, is there anything else He wouldn't gladly and freely do for us? And who would dare tangle with God by messing with one of God's chosen? Who would dare even to point a finger? The One who died for us— who was raised to life for us! —is in the presence of God at this very moment sticking up for us. Do you think anyone is going to be able to drive a wedge between us and Christ's love for us? There is no way! Not trouble, not hard times, not hatred, not hunger, not homelessness, not bullying threats, not backstabbing, not even the worst sins listed in Scripture: They kill us in cold blood because they hate you. We're sitting ducks; they pick us off one by one. None of this fazes us because Jesus loves us. I'm absolutely convinced that nothing—nothing living or dead, angelic or demonic, today or tomorrow, high or low, thinkable or unthinkable—absolutely nothing can get between us and God's love because of the way that Jesus our Master has embraced us."*

These several verses in Romans are some of my absolute favorite verses in the entire Bible. These words are life-changing and faith-altering declarations from God about your life, your future, and how God sees you. God is on your side, and with God on your side, you shall not lose. He has given you victory over the enemy; over the power of sin and death; over fear, panic, anxiety and depression; over hatred; over judgment and condemnation. You are more than a conqueror through Jesus because He loves you so much that He gave you His power and provision to overcome any obstacle you may face. Jesus was made to be sin, so yours are now forgiven, once and for all. No matter where you have been, no matter what you have done, and no matter how many times you may have done it, God loves you and accepts you. Now it is time for you to accept it. You read the words above. God did not hesitate to put everything on the line for you. He embraced your conditions. He exposed Himself to the worst of humanity and Satan by sending Jesus to the earth in the form of a man to free you and forgive you. There is nothing He will not freely and joyfully do for you to help you, forgive you, restore you and heal you. Please understand, God cherishes you with passion and excitement. He created you on purpose. He loves you unconditionally, and there is nothing that can drive a wedge between you and His love. Say it with me one last time, "I am God's masterpiece!"

In your life, you may have been unfaithful, but you have never been and will never be unloved by God. That amazing truth reveals an incredible understanding to the following revelations for your life:

> In your life, you may have been untrue, but you have never and will never be unloved by God!

> In your life, you may have been unreliable, but you have never and will never be unloved by God!

> In your life, you may have been unholy, but you have never and will never be unloved by God!

> In your life, you may have been unworthy, but you have never and will never be unloved by God!

CHAPTER 15

In your life, you may have been unwanted,
but you have never and will never be
unloved by God!

In your life, you may have been uncertain,
but you have never and will never be
unloved by God!

In your life, you may have been undecided,
but you have never and will never be
unloved by God!

In your life, you may have been unruly, but
you have never and will never be unloved
by God!

In your life, you may have been unbelievable,
but you have never and will never be
unloved by God!

In your life, you may have been unclean, but
you have never and will never be unloved
by God!

In your life, you may have been underneath,
but you have never and will never be
unloved by God!

In your life, you may have been unforgiving,
but you have never and will never be
unloved by God!

In your life, you may have been ungodly, but
you have never and will never be unloved
by God!

In your life, you may have been unjust, but
you have never and will never be unloved
by God!

CHERISHED, VALUED, LOVED

In your life, you may have been unwise, but you have never and will never be unloved by God!

In your life, you may have been unreasonable, but you have never and will never be unloved by God!

In your life, you may have been unknown, but you have never and will never be unloved by God!

In your life, you may have been unstable, but you have never and will never be unloved by God!

In your life, you may have been unrighteous, but you have never and will never be unloved by God!

You never have been and you never will be unloved by God. Do not ever let anyone, including yourself, tell you that you are anything other than God's cherished masterpiece.

What Are You Thinking?

THE MISSING PEACE

What Are You Thinking?

Proverbs 23:7 — *"For as he thinks in his heart, so is he."*

If you have ever read King Solomon's book of wisdom, you know there are many great truths he revealed that are still incredibly relevant to our lives today. However, this is truly one of the simplest, yet most deeply profound scriptures in the book of Proverbs. If you take a moment to mull over it, you will recognize its truth. You most likely see it in yourself and have seen it in others. Your life goes the way your thinking goes. Did you know the average person thinks between 50,000 to 70,000 thoughts per day? That is 35 to 48 thoughts per minute. Obviously, out of those thousands of daily thoughts, many of them are fleeting and irrelevant. Something comes in our mind one second and is gone the next. Many thoughts barely even register in your mind and are not worth your time or effort to meditate on. Here is the important question though: "What are your predominant thoughts?" Have you ever taken a moment to analyze what the narrative is within your head? To a large extent, your thoughts shape your reality. Your predominant thoughts will give birth to your emotions and feelings, and ultimately determine how you respond to circumstances, situations and people in your life. Many people dedicate significant amounts of time mentally and emotionally to what others think about them, while giving very little time to what is going on inside their own heads. While other people's opinions about us may affect how we feel, those opinions are not the most important issue. The scripture above did not say that what another person thinks about you, so are you. It does not really matter what other people think about you. Truly, your own thoughts about yourself matter.

What do you think about yourself and your life?
What do you think about God?
What do you think about your future?
What do you think about your family?
What do you think about your spouse, or future spouse?
What do you think about your school or city?
What do you think about your job or career?
What do you think about your church?

Your thoughts determine everything about you. They affect your beliefs, your expectation, your mood, your responses, your choices and your words. Your predominant thoughts will decide how you perceive the events of your life. Right or wrong, your perception is your reality. If the theme of your mind is negative, life will show you plenty of things to justify that negativity. If you live gratefully, you will find plenty of things throughout your day to be thankful for. If the narrative within your psyche is one of complaining, rest assured you will find plenty of things to criticize.

Think of this like you think of nature. Everything in nature is produced from within itself. An apple has seeds within it that can be planted to produce an apple tree, which will produce more apples. The same goes with oranges, limes, animals and even humans. The seed to produce more of the same is always within itself. Have you ever thought about a bad situation and the more you meditated on it, the worse it seemed? Have you ever had one negative thing happen during your day, allowed that negativity to fester within your head, and it ruined the rest of your day? You hear people say all the time that they had the worst day. I often wonder if they really had a terrible day, or if they just had a terrible few minutes that they gave unnecessary authority over the rest of their day. Whether positive or negative, if you allow a prolonged thought to sit in your mind and you dwell on it for a significant amount of time, your mind will inevitably produce more and more similar thoughts. If positive, your thoughts will be ruled by hope, faith and excitement. If negative, your thoughts will be ruled by anxiety, fear and apathy. So many people live their lives focused on what they do not have, what they wanted and did not get, what went wrong, or the life they are not living. Year after year goes by and this focus never produces what they want in their life. Why? Because the seed to produce what they want is not there. You cannot plant a seed you do not have; therefore, you can let your thoughts control you, or you can control them. **When you take control of your thinking, you take control of your life.**

There is an interesting story in Genesis 20 about Abraham, the father of faith, as he travels with his wife Sarah into the land of Gerar. They are foreigners in King Abimelech's region. As they settle down to dwell in the land, Abraham tells people Sarah is his sister, not his wife. The king takes Sarah with the intentions of having adult relations with her until God speaks to him in a dream and tells him the truth of who she is. King Abimelech is rightfully upset and disturbed that Abraham would set him up to commit what was considered a mortal sin in those days. The king never intended to wrong God or Abraham. He was lied to, and this lie led him to the brink of disaster. As you would expect, immediately upon waking from his dream, he summons Abraham to his presence to explain his actions. Here is the interaction:

187

Verse 10 (Message) — *"Abimelech went on to Abraham, 'Whatever were you thinking of when you did this thing?'"*

Verse 11 (NKJV) — *"And Abraham said, 'Because I thought, surely the fear of God is not in this place; and they will kill me on account of my wife.'"*

The king had every right to question Abraham in this moment. Abraham almost cost him his life and his kingdom. You can see in verse 11 that Abraham made this foolish decision due to a faulty assumption based on fear. It is easy in life to forget that God is on your side. It is easy to assume incorrectly about people, places and things. It is easy to think and presume the worst in society. It is easy to lose control of your thoughts and be ruled by doubt, insecurity and fear. It is easy to make bad choices in relationships, finances, business or health because of bad thinking. Naturally, those bad choices only produce more bad thinking. I imagine that every one of us has had a moment of frustration where someone said to us, "What were you thinking?" or maybe you have said it to yourself. "My God, what was I thinking?" or "I never thought...." But you could have! Let me take it one step further: not only could you have, you should have thought through your choices and decisions.

The reality of our lives today is there is simply no excuse for ignorance. There is far too much information and resource available at our fingertips to go through life uninformed. In fact, Proverbs 1:20 says that wisdom cries out to us in life. Everywhere you turn, there is wisdom. The question is whether you have a mental environment established where it can flow into your life. Wrong assumptions and ignorance lead to terrible mistakes. Mistakes are costly and someone must pay for them. The causes of mistakes typically sound like this: "I didn't know," "I didn't think," or "I didn't care." The best time to correct mistakes is before they are made. The easiest way to do so is to get control of your thinking.

Thinking vs. Thoughts

One observation to point out in the story above is that Abraham thought when he should have been thinking. In fact, his lack of thinking almost caused mass destruction and chaos for himself, his wife, King Abimelech and his kingdom. Because of the flood of thoughts that enter your mind daily, being ruled by them becomes a potentially dangerous way to live. That is why it is so important to think. Thinking is much more than a thought. Thinking involves information. Thinking involves humility and an understanding that you need wisdom and counsel spoken into your life. Thinking involves discernment. Thinking involves seeking truth from outside sources. Thinking involves intentionally filtering the healthy thoughts from the harmful ones.

To truly obtain peace in your mind, you must begin to sift through the negative, unhealthy, and even tormenting thoughts in an effort to get them out of your thinking so your life can produce the peace you so desire. Let's look at some destructive thought types that the Bible instructs us to be aware of, so you can usurp them before they control your thought processes.

1 Childish Thoughts

1 Corinthians 13:11 — *"When I was a child, I spoke as a child, I understood as a child, I thought as a child; but when I became a man, I put away childish things."*

Childish thoughts tend to be uninformed, overly emotional, inconsistent and often very selfish. Childish thoughts are exactly like children. They need wisdom, discipline and correction. So do your thoughts. A fantastic decision to make within your mind is to guard against childish thoughts and not respond to them. God created us to go from being a child to an adult – immature to mature – but maturity is not defined by age. Maturity is defined by your behavior, not by how long you have walked the earth. Behavior is a choice, and so is maturity. The Apostle Paul shows us he put away childish behavior. What that tells me is he identified it, addressed it within his own mind, and corrected it by completely removing it from his life. He made the decision to grow up, to be mentally mature. Paul recognized he needed to get better in life so he could advance further in his God-given calling. If Paul, one of the greatest men to ever live, needed to do this, most likely we all do as well.

189

2 Foolish Thoughts

Proverbs 24:9 — *"The devising of foolishness is sin. And the scoffer is an abomination to men."*

The very definition of a fool is one who lacks forethought. A fool is a person who does not take time to think about their thoughts. That is what happened to Abraham in the story you read above, and it took God intervening to avoid a disaster. Fools simply react to whatever comes into their mind. We all have foolish thoughts,

"Be angry, and do not sin."

but you do not have to speak them, believe them or act upon them. Foolishness leads to sin, and this scripture points out that many fools become scoffers. A scoffer is one who mocks people, belittles them, and tears them down with their words. They think they know everything about everyone. They are always the expert. In fact, Proverbs 12:15 says, *"The way of a fool is right in his own eyes, but he who heeds counsel is wise."* A great life is built on wisdom, but it can only be received when it is welcomed. Counsel can only enter your mind if you take time to think about your thoughts. A true sign of maturity and wisdom is the acceptance that you are not as wise as you need to be. Your thoughts are not always the right thoughts. Your thoughts do not always need to be spoken. Your opinion is not always the correct opinion, nor does it always need to be given. A fool will reject wisdom through the unrecognized act of pride while simultaneously watching their life fall apart. Proverbs 10:21 says, *"Fools die for want of wisdom."* Open up your mind to allowing wisdom to enter your heart and build your life accordingly. You can avoid foolishness with foresight, prudence and planning. Don't just react. Don't just respond with the first thing that pops into your mind. Don't live your life thinking you know everything. Don't live like a fool.

190

3 Angry Thoughts

Ephesians 4:26 — *"Be angry, and do not sin."*

All of us get angry. The prophets in the Bible got angry. The disciples got angry. God the Father even displayed anger toward sin and injustice. Anger is inevitable and natural. Anger can be healthy and even inspire great change when properly addressed and controlled. However, anger is dangerously toxic if you do not deal with it correctly.

The Lord is telling you to be angry, but not to allow your anger to turn to sin. Jesus was angry on several occasions in the Gospels, but his anger always produced justice, never malice. Jesus controlled His anger to accomplish what He needed to accomplish. Too often, people lose their tempers in anger, and the problem they are upset about does not get addressed in a healthy manner, if at all. Quite regularly, the lost temper moves the focus off the issue and places it on the out-of-control behavior that is being displayed. People who lose their temper end up saying things they did not mean. Things that should have never been said.

Unbridled anger produces wrath. Wrath produces destruction. Anger turned to wrath never leads to solutions. Unresolved problems create anxiety, stress and frustration. That is why in verse 29 of this same chapter in Ephesians we are told to never let any corrupt word proceed out of our mouths. Rather, we are to use words to uplift and edify those we are conversing with. You cannot encourage someone if you are out of control. In fact, verse 21 states, *"Let all bitterness, wrath, anger, clamor and evil speaking be put away from you with all malice."* Just like childish thoughts, we are directed to "put away" the words and damaging emotions that develop when anger within us gets out of control. In fact, the author says to put it away with all malice. I interpret that as saying that I should be angry at allowing my anger to be out of control.

191

People tell me all time they cannot control their temper. My response is, "Yes you can. You control it all the time. If not, you would be in prison. You control it at work. You control it in society. You control it every day of your life. You just don't control it with the people you have lost respect for."

No one controls you, except you. Stop lying to yourself that you cannot control your temper. What I am about to say is extremely blunt, but please understand I say it because I care about your future. Grow up! Get yourself under control and knock it off. Losing your temper has caused you enough turmoil. It is time to make a change. My dad said that to me once. I never lost my temper again. You make the decision to let your anger produce positive change or cause harm. It is up to you.

4 Evil Thoughts

Matthew 15:19 — *"For out of the heart proceed evil thoughts."*

Jesus says your heart will produce evil thoughts if you are not careful. What is in your heart? Remember God tells you repeatedly in His Word to guard your heart. You do not want to allow childish behavior, foolish thoughts, and undealt with anger to corrupt your heart. Philippians 4:7 says, *"And the peace of God, which surpasses all understanding, will guard your hearts and minds through Christ Jesus."* This is truly one of the great scriptures in the Bible that shows the extent of the power of God's peace. Peace is not just an emotion or a state of mind, it is a weapon given to you by God to help you guard your heart and mind. Please do not forget, when God declared peace on earth, one of the declarations He made was that He was doing all kinds of good things for His children. How do you counter evil? With good. Good overcomes evil when the good is from God. The peace of God will manifest within your soul because Jesus is the Prince of Peace, and He lives inside you. Evil thoughts come into your mind to separate you from God, His Word, and His promise of peace. The easiest defense against this is to be aware of it and not allow these thoughts to stay with you. It is unavoidable to have them, but you do not have to keep them. You do not have to accept them. You are the ruler of your predominant thoughts. You control your mind. **You decide what thoughts will be given citizenship to live inside your soul and which ones will be expelled.**

That is why it is so important for you to have a relationship with the Word of God. Every scripture in the Bible is written for inspiration, wisdom, hope, edification, and the renewing of your mind to bring you into a place of peace. The more you know God's Word, the more His Word will produce the life-giving thoughts you need to build your life on. Hebrews 4:12 says, *"For the Word of God is living and powerful, and sharper than any two-edged sword, piercing even to the division of soul and spirit, and of joints and marrow, and is a discerner of the thoughts and intents of the heart."* There is truly nothing like the Word of God. His Word is alive, it is powerful, and it is completely relevant to your everyday life. It breathes life into your soul, energy into your mind, and clarity into your thoughts. One of its most vital qualities is that its wisdom corrects your thinking. As the scripture stated, it discerns your thoughts. That means that God's Word says "yes" to the right thoughts and "no" to the wrong ones. The Word will turn dark to light, hate to love, evil to good, fear to faith, ignorance to wisdom, and anxiety to peace.

Psalm 1:2 — *"But his delight is in the law of the Lord, and in His law he meditates day and night."*

Joshua 1:8 — *"This Book of the Law shall not depart from your mouth, but you shall meditate in it day and night, that you may observe to do according to all that is written in it. For then you will make your way prosperous, and then you will have good success."*

Both the above scriptures use the word "meditate" in connection to God's Word. To meditate is to think about something consistently and continually. First, you cannot think about what you do not know, so knowing God's Word is of utmost importance. Second, the more you know, the more you will do. Right thinking produces right living. Right living produces right results. Right results produce peace. Right thinking comes from aligning your thoughts with God's thoughts. God's thoughts come from His Word. You read it in the above scripture from Joshua. God's Word produces success and prosperity in your life. That is who God is and that is why Jesus came to the earth. He gave you His Word because He wants you to have a happy, fulfilled, victorious and peaceful life as a result of all the good He does for you. Every word in the Bible is there to make your life better. Every command is given out of love for you to inspire a good way to live. Every thought God provokes is meant to correct, encourage and help you. His ways are the right ways. I regularly tell our church, "If you want God's results, just do it God's way." God is not complicated. His results are amazing and are realized by simply living out His Word. That life starts by allowing His thoughts to become your predominant thoughts. It all starts with having a relationship with His Word, the Bible.

193

I am very aware that many people are intimidated by reading the Bible. They do not know where to start or what to read. The first tip I can give you is to just start. I tell people all the time to give the Bible twenty minutes out of your day. Twenty minutes to change your life! You can do twenty minutes. You may be busy, but you are not that busy. Everyone can find twenty minutes in their day. It is just a matter of priority. You can wake up a bit earlier, carve out some time during your lunch break, or just binge one less episode of whatever you are currently watching at night. Everyone has twenty minutes. If changing your life is important to you, you will make time for it. Nowadays, I usually tell people to download the YouVersion Bible application on their smart device. It is free and is truly one of the greatest blessings given to the body of Christ in my generation. YouVersion has an abundance of daily Bible reading plans to start your journey. It also provides numerous topical devotionals to help address specific situations or issues you may be dealing with. The key is to do it though, and to stay consistent. I promise, if you will give God twenty minutes out of your day, six months from now you will be happier than you ever have been.

Let's go back to the book of Philippians, where the Apostle Paul tells us God's peace will guard our hearts and minds. That is verse 7. Immediately in verse 8, he says, *"Finally, brethren, whatever things are true, whatever things are noble, whatever things are just, whatever things are pure, whatever things are lovely, whatever things are of good report, if there is any virtue and if there is anything praiseworthy - mediate on these things."* This is quite simple really. Paul tells you exactly what kinds of thoughts should become your predominant thoughts so the peace of God can guard your mind.

Meditate on thoughts that are:

■ True — Thoughts That Are
1 Sincere, Upright and Honest

John 8:32 — *"And you shall know the truth, and the truth shall make you free."*

A peaceful mind is a free mind. A peaceful mind is free from confusion, doubt, lies and distrust. Only a mind that is empowered with truth can actually be peacefully free. The truth can only set you free if the truth is received and believed. God's Word is the truth. Meditate on what is true so you can be free!

■ Noble — Thoughts That Are Honest,
2 Reputable and Dignified

Nobility is a great virtue. A noble person is a good person. You can count on and rely upon a person of honesty and dignity. I imagine we have all had encounters with people that left us with a bad taste in our mouths, so to speak. You could just tell there was something not right about their words or intentions. What happens in moments like that? You are cautious and without trust. Focus your mind on thoughts and people that have a good reputation.

■ Just — Things That Indicate They are
3 Right and Conformed to Righteousness

You know right from wrong. We all do. You know when you should or should not do or say something. The question is, will you act upon what is right or what is wrong? All that behavior starts in your head. If you allow the wrong thoughts to linger in your mind, eventually you will exhibit corresponding words and actions.

■ Pure — To Be Innocent or
4 Without Blame

None of us are perfect in this area, but every person can take responsibility for their lives. Right now, you can commit to be the owner of your life and your future. We see people throughout society live their lives blaming everything on everyone else, while never taking account of their own actions. If you are wrong, take responsibility for it and get it fixed. Make the changes in your life that you already know you need to change. That is the way to a good life.

5   ◼ Lovely — Thoughts That Are Acceptable and Pleasing to the Lord

This is quite easy really. God is good and He does good; therefore, if you are going to think thoughts that are pleasing to the Lord, think good ones. Think about encouraging someone. Think about forgiving those who have wronged you. Think about ways you can be a blessing to your loved ones. Think about doing a great job at work. Think about planning nice moments for your spouse. Think about what you have instead of what you do not have. Think about ways you can be generous. Think about all the times God has blessed you. Think about ways you can make the world a better place, or at least your world.

6   ◼ Good Report — Thoughts That Are Praiseworthy and Honorable

I quit watching the news years ago. Not because I did not want to be informed, but rather because there were too many bad reports. The local and the national news was filled with negativity and everything that was wrong in life. I found myself angry, anxious, and stressed out every night. Here is the ridiculous part about it: most of the stories had zero impact on my life. I was getting all worked up over things I had no control of and had little effect on my reality. The world is filled with negativity, pessimism and bad news. You must protect your mind from being filled with them. Have you ever thought about what you watch on television, what music you listen to and what news you read? Is it constructive or destructive? What about the people you follow on social media? Is what you are seeing online building up your spirit and bringing joy or is it tearing you apart with turmoil and frustration?

Quite some time ago, I assessed what I was inputting into my soul and it was not good. I was watching suspense and mystery shows and movies. I was listening to super negative hard rock music. My favorite bands were Disturbed and Godsmack. I mean no offense to them – in fact I really liked them – but their music was not doing me any good mentally. You do not need to Google their music to know it is not exactly uplifting. All you need to do is look at the band names to know. I do not watch horror movies or anything with spirits or witchcraft. Take a day or two and really think about what you are feeding yourself via television, books, articles, and movies and ask yourself whether it is helping your mental state of mind.

Remember, your life is a reflection of your predominant thoughts. It is so important to take time to think. You need to allow yourself to filter out the wrong thoughts and digest the right ones. If the body does not digest its food, it will not receive the nutrients it needs to extract from it. The same is true with your thoughts. If your mind is constantly blocked or clouded with the wrong things, you cannot extrapolate the wisdom and understanding you need to maintain your peace and keep a healthy focus. Not every thought is a God-thought, so giving yourself time to think and protect what you allow into your mind will help you find the right ones and get rid of the wrong ones. This simple and necessary exercise will help you keep the peace in your mind.

197

Winning the Battle in Your Mind

Winning the Battle in Your Mind

When I was a child, my parents significantly guarded what my sister and I could watch on television. They never allowed us to view anything with witchcraft, spells or something of a sinister nature. Occasionally, my friends at school would make fun of me for not having seen certain Disney movies, or other famous shows or cartoons they were all discussing. As time went by though, i realized there was a stark difference between myself and many of my classmates and friends. I never spoke of nightmares or being scared. I vividly remember having a friend stay at my house one weekend and he feared the boogie man in the closet. I honestly did not even know what he was talking about. I just remember thinking, there's just clothes and shoes in there. Nothing to be afraid of. I never had nightmares. I was not afraid of the dark or nervous about random noises. I did not even know I was supposed to be anxious about any of it in the first place. I may have not seen some of the regular movies and famous shows my friends saw, but like many kids that grew up in the 80s and 90s, I woke up every Saturday morning to watch cartoons. My favorites were the superheroes. Nothing greater than saving the world, right? Also, Batman is the greatest without question! Anyway, back in those days, a common theme in cartoons was the villain trying to exact mind control over innocent victims to influence everyone to execute their evil plan of world domination. For some reason, those always caught my attention. I never liked the idea of someone hypnotizing me, wrongly influencing me, or manipulating me into some foolish behavior or belief system. In cartoons, it is funny and of course the bad guy never wins, but in real life, having a mind that is out of control or ruled by the wrong forces can be extremely detrimental to your overall wellbeing. Who is controlling your mind right now?

No one other than you should be in control of your mind. Just like your heart, there is a daily battle taking place for control of your mind. Here is the good news: you can, and you will now start winning this battle. The devil wants to take control and grip you with negativity, anxiety and fear in order to keep you from living with the peace God has given you. Your victory in this daily battle is crucial because the mind is incredibly powerful. You can talk yourself in or out of just about anything. The steady flow of thinking is a thick filter between your thoughts and feelings, your head and your heart. Peace or turmoil rests on what is in your mind. Your predominant thoughts create what will become the issues of your heart. The issues of your heart determine the boundaries of your life, your daily decisions, and the direction of your future. Out of the abundance of your heart, you will speak. The Bible states that life and death is in the power of the tongue. If life and death is in the power of the tongue, and what you speak starts with what you think, we can only conclude that life and death is in the power of your mind. Deuteronomy 30:19 says, *"I call heaven and earth as witnesses today against you, that I have set before you life and death, blessing and cursing; therefore choose life, that both you and your descendants may live."* You see, God ties life and blessing together into a choice you make. Your choices not only determine the happiness and success of your life, but Deuteronomy highlights a reality most people are already aware of: your choices also affect your descendants' lives. Your life will set the example that your children and your children's children will follow. You will successfully choose blessing by successfully winning the battle for control of your mind.

John 16:33 (NIV) — *"I have told you these things, so that in Me you may have peace. In this world you will have trouble. But take heart! I have overcome the world."*

Jesus draws a very clear line in the sand with His words in this great scripture. With Him, you will have peace. In the world, you will have trouble. Trouble is undeniable. Every person on this planet will deal with challenge, obstacle, change, hurt and pain. Negativity sometimes seems to abound and multiply in life. You must determine to not allow those troubles to defeat you. Jesus has given you the power to overcome them. You can do all things through Christ who gives you strength. You can do the hard things. You can do the painful things. You can do the exhausting and overwhelming things. But you cannot give in to the trouble. The first place that trouble tries to overcome you is in your mind. The attack will always start in your thoughts. Philippians 4:5 states, *"Be anxious for nothing."* One of the definitions of the word anxious is to be troubled. I used to hate this scripture. How could God expect me to be anxious for nothing, to not be troubled? I remember reading this over and over as a young adult and actually feeling anxiety about the fact that I could not live up to this verse. Then, I would condemn myself for being anxious over a scripture that says to not be anxious. I know it sounds ridiculous, but I really would fret over it. It just did not add up for me, and I knew God's Word. I knew He did not give me His Word to frustrate me.

In my 20s and early 30s, I really struggled with my thoughts. My mind would fixate on an issue, big or small, and would run wild. It usually happened at night when I was trying to sleep and get rest. I would lay in bed and conjure up every horrible situation you can imagine. Of course, none of them ever happened. Anxiety would fill my soul. I even had times where I could literally feel my heart beating on the pillow. Has that ever happened to you? You can be perfectly fine all day, and then your mind starts racing and before you know it, your thoughts are full-blown crazy.

2 TIMOTHY 1:7

"For God has not given us a spirit of fear, but of power and of love and of a sound mind."

This is a very famous scripture. Many Christians quote this scripture daily in their prayers. In fact, I declare this over my children every night when we pray together at bedtime. One day a few years back, I decided to do a deep study of this verse to discover what God was truly saying here. The first thing I want to point out to you is God has not given you a spirit of fear. Please understand, if God did not give you something, you do not have to accept it. He did not give you fear, or any of fear's friends like anxiety, depression, worry or hatred. It is time to learn how to reject it. It is time to win the battle of your mind. He gave you power. The word power means strength to overcome cowardice. You also know from earlier readings in this book that the power of God is His faith. Faith overcomes fear. He gave you His love which is perfect. The Bible says the perfect love of God casts out all fear. It was the love of God that inspired Him to send Jesus to the earth so you can be saved and live in peace and goodwill all the days of your life. The third statement is the one that changed my life. He gave you a sound mind. What does that mean? The phrase "a sound mind" means to correct, to make sober, and to discipline the mind to maintain sound judgment. The heart must be guarded, but the mind needs to be disciplined. The disciplining of your mind is completely up to you. The Lord has given you His power, His love and His peace to enable you to do it, but you must take the appropriate action. Discipline is a personal decision one makes about their lifestyle. No one can choose discipline for another person. God cannot discipline you to eat healthy or exercise, and neither can your friends, family or doctor. Only you can discipline your mind. No one can do it for you. At times, discipline is hard, particularly at the beginning. Discipline is daily. It never stops and it is all encompassing, but it is worth it. A disciplined mind is a sound mind, a controlled mind and a free mind. A disciplined mind produces healthy emotions and sound judgment. A disciplined mind results in a peace-filled life. The easy choice is to keep letting your mind be ruled by whatever goes on around you, but easy will not get you where you want to go. Yes, discipline can be challenging. Are you going to view the challenge as obstacle, or as opportunity? If you see it only as an obstacle, you will not take the necessary steps to overcome it. But, if you focus your mind on the reward that lies beyond the obstacle, you will do whatever it takes to maximize this opportunity to win the battle in your mind and be at peace.

Overcoming Strongholds

2 Corinthians 10:4-6 — *"For the weapons of our warfare are not carnal but mighty in God for pulling down strongholds, casting down arguments and every high thing that exalts itself against the knowledge of God, bringing every thought into captivity to the obedience of Christ, and being ready to punish all disobedience when your obedience is fulfilled."*

These verses tell you just about everything you need to know about disciplining and taking control of your mind. The scripture first highlights that the goal of the enemy is to establish mental strongholds that are contrary to what God has planned for you. I find it fascinating that the author chose this word. A stronghold is a well-fortified place used in combat to protect who and what you are fighting for. It is a fortress. Do you have any strongholds in your mind? If so, are they good or bad? Quite often, the stronghold is a result of what I call preprogrammed thinking. These are the thoughts and beliefs about yourself and your future that you were raised with or picked up as you matured. Too often, this type of thinking is negative in the fact that we allowed inadequacies, failures and insecurities to define our outlook on life. Year after year goes by and these strongholds are left without challenge in your heart and mind. As time passes, they continue to produce exactly what they are. The feeling of inadequacy causes you to not go back to school to get your master's degree or apply for that promotion you know you are qualified for. The feeling of brokenness causes you to sabotage relationships because you are convinced, either consciously or subconsciously, that you do not deserve to be happy. The feeling of pessimism produces a fatalistic perception that life is against you and things are not going to work out well. You do not have to continue to live unaware of what is destroying your belief system, your attitude and your decision making. I will tell you now that preprogrammed thinking is the hardest to discipline, but it can be done. You can now learn how to tear down destructive strongholds and establish productive ones. To do so, you just need to understand the process.

203

■ It Starts With
1 a Thought

You read in the above scripture to be ready to bring every thought into captivity to the obedience of Christ. Our human nature, combined with the imperfections of life and society, will always produce thoughts that are contrary to God's Word. They can be thoughts of anger, lust, fear, greed, selfishness and much more. The thought usually just sounds like a suggestion. What if? Why not? No one will even notice. What does it matter anyway? Most likely, some of these thoughts have come into your mind as you have read this book or maybe even this chapter. I can't do this. This isn't true. There is just no way. This is too difficult. The sin Adam and Eve committed in the garden of Eden started with just a thought as well, when the serpent asked Eve why God had said they could not eat from every tree in the garden. All it took was the simple question, "why?" Isn't that amazing? The wrong thought left to fester in your mind can cause incredible damage. That is why you should be ready to discipline those types of thoughts. Just get rid of them. Eve's response to the serpent should have been, "Because God commanded it." That's it. The entire experience would have been over with if Adam or Eve had been mentally disciplined and not allowed the thought to be anything more than exactly what it was, a thought. But that is not what happened.

■ It Continues With
2 a Contradiction

The wrong thought left unpunished will produce a contradictory mindset. Here is truly where the stronghold starts to fortify. The scripture above describes this as *every high thing that exalts itself against the knowledge of God.* Once the enemy gets you dwelling on a certain thought, he brings the contradiction. For example, I just spent four chapters telling you God sees you as a masterpiece. I imagine many of you had contradictory thoughts running through your mind as you read through those pages. The enemy does not want you to believe what God believes about you. He does not want you to think that you can overcome anxiety, depression and fear. He will do everything in his power to fool you into believing you are helpless and hopeless in the struggle to be free and at peace. The contradiction may come, but the contradiction is a lie. It is a lie created to deceive you and put you into bondage within a fortress of misery. It happened to Adam and Eve. Eve told the serpent God said they would die if they ate the fruit from the one tree. Satan responded by telling them that they would surely not die. He exalted his word above the Word of God, and they fell for it.

God says you are healed. Satan will tell you that you are sick. God says you are forgiven. Satan will try to tell you that you have sinned too much. God says you are restored. Satan will tell you that you are damaged goods. God says you are blessed. Satan says nothing is ever good enough. Just because the contradiction enters your mind does not mean it is true, nor does it mean you have to believe it. You must determine to maintain control of your thoughts, not the devil, not your ex, not your former boss, not the national news, and not anyone or anything else that does not have your best interest in mind. If a thought does not agree with God, it should not be allowed to agree with you.

■ It Establishes Itself
3 With Arguments

A stronghold is only as powerful as its defense system. Within your mind, the stronghold solidifies through winning the argument. This happens when the wrong thought is given permission to run wild in your mind, while empowering the contradiction to create false imaginations or reasonings that you allow or justify. At the point the contradiction is justified, you have a stronghold that will influence your behavior until the stronghold is defeated. That is exactly what happened to Eve. The serpent told her if she ate the fruit she would be like God. She then looked at the tree and convinced herself it was good to eat even though God had told her it was not. You know the rest of the story. She and Adam both ate, and they did not become like God. Quite the contrary. Eve went from a thought, to a contradiction, to an argument that resulted in a stronghold that changed the course of humanity forever. What happened to Adam and Eve? They allowed an outside influence to win an argument in their minds that should have never even been allowed to make it past the initial thought.

Your mind is a battlefield. Our scripture reference above concludes by directing us to be ready to punish all disobedience until obedience is fulfilled. **The daily battle for your mind is won by exacting the necessary discipline and correction of your thoughts until your thinking aligns with who God says you are.** Your life will transform as you renew your mind and reject the ways of the world. The more you correct the wrong thoughts and empower the right ones, the more peace will replace anxiety, joy will replace sadness, faith will replace fear, and so on and so forth. Do not undervalue the benefits of a disciplined mind. The question isn't whether or not you are capable of disciplining your mind. The question is whether you will do what it takes to be disciplined. Discipline is determining to say yes mentally, emotionally and physically to the right things and no to the wrong things, even when you do not want to. It is determining within yourself to make short term sacrifices to achieve a desired, long term outcome. You are going to have to decide you want a mind ruled by peace more than the world wants to keep you fastened to anxiety and fear.

The war being waged is a war for truth. When truth is really true, it will set you free, but far too often, we allow thoughts, opinions and experiences to be labeled as true within our belief system without them actually being true. Here is the problem with that: if you have accepted something as truth, it is in fact true to you, whether or not it is true in reality. The enemy's goal is to influence you into accepting falsities as truth. At the point you have accepted a lie as truth, you have lost the battle of your mind. God has empowered you with His Word, His promises, His peace and His identity for you to build your life on what He has declared is the truth – regardless of your past experience, what you have read or heard, or what people have said. What God has declared and said is the truth, and that is the truth that the enemy will always try to contradict. That is also the truth that will set you free!

Far too many people live believing things about their lives that are not true. It is true to you because you believe it, but that does not mean it is true. It becomes your reality, but it does not have to stay that way. What has taken place in your mind is that a contradiction has become a stronghold, and that contradiction needs to be confronted, and in fact contradicted itself. Maybe you have believed a "truth" that you are not good enough. Maybe you have believed a "truth" that you do not deserve to be happy or prosperous or successful. Maybe you have believed a "truth" that you are broken beyond repair. You have accepted "truth," except the "truth" you have accepted is a lie. Assigning the word truth to a narrative does not make the narrative true; consequently, the necessity of identifying truth is of the utmost importance.

"Let me ask you a question though: do you ever argue with yourself?..."

Please understand the enemy is a liar and an accuser. I have found he typically accuses us in our weakness. We all have strengths and weaknesses. He does not accuse you in your strength because he knows you will immediately reject and overcome it. He accuses you in your weakness in an attempt to fortify the weakness at such a level that it overcomes you. He wants the weakness to become a stronghold for lies. It may be an insecurity. It might be in an area of sin that we have not dealt with. Maybe he floods our thoughts with regret from mistakes made in the past. As long as we allow him, he will accuse us in that depression, fear or anxiety. Regardless of what the accusation is, this is something we all will deal with. Like in a court of law, Satan will charge you with negativity, blame or fault to convict and sentence your future into bondage to that life. All these accusations start in your mind – and you can overcome any of them because Satan has no rightful power over you.

Revelation 12:10-11 — *"...for the accuser of our brethren, who accused them before our God day and night, has been cast down. And they overcame him by the blood of the Lamb and by the word of their testimony."*

Isaiah 54:17 (AMP) — *"'No weapon that is formed against you will succeed; and every tongue that rises against you in judgment you will condemn. This [peace, righteousness, security, and triumph over opposition] is the heritage of the servants of the Lord, and this is their vindication from Me,' says the Lord."*

I want to call attention to a theme within these two scriptures. The first one is one I have already discussed in this book, and that is that Jesus has given you authority over the enemy. The second one is what we will focus on now. Both reference the fact that you overcome through your words. You must condemn within yourself any word spoken that is a false accusation. The verdict you allow into your mind to define your words and your life must be based on fact, on truth, and never on lies. A verdict is issued in a court of law after opposing attorneys have argued their cases. Therein lies the key to winning the battle in your mind. You must win the argument in your mind.

So many people are great at arguing. We will argue politics. We will argue who the greatest quarterback of all time is. We will argue about our favorite restaurants, movies or cities to visit. We will argue with our coworkers, friends, people we have never met on social media, kids, and even our spouses. I know people who look for arguments and appear to enjoy them. Most arguments are inconsequential and a waste of our emotional time and energy. Let me ask you a question though: do you ever argue with yourself? I bet you do, but most people who struggle with anxiety, worry or depression are fighting the wrong fight. You must train yourself to win the argument in your mind based on the truth of who God says you are and the life He says you can enjoy living. Like the petulant child who will go to any extreme to get what they want, you must be willing to do the same to overcome the false truths that have defined your frame of mind and influenced your reality for far too long. If the accusation is that you are a loser; but Jesus says you are a winner. Who are you going to believe? You are strong in the Lord, not weak. You are blessed, not cursed. You are forgiven, not shamed.

The accuser says you are unworthy, but God says you are loved unconditionally. You are loved so much that He sent Jesus to die on the cross for you. His love for you is unrelenting and unwavering, but you must decide what you are going to believe and what stronghold you are going to build within your thoughts. The most determined person usually wins the argument. Your desire must be set to accept nothing but God's truth declared for your life. You will argue with anyone and everyone about things that do not really matter, but you will not argue with yourself about who you are as a peace-declared child of the most high God. It is time now, right now, to start winning the argument in your mind so you can redefine how you think, how you believe and how you speak about your life, your future, your family, your passions and your desires. This is the moment to expose the lie with the truth. It is time for us to accept the verdict of freedom God gave us over the accuser. You are not a victim. You are a victor. You have the mind of Christ. You are not bound. You are free because Jesus has declared freedom over you. **When you win the battle of your mind, you win control over your life.**

209

Positive or Negative?

Positive or Negative?

My wife and I had a whirlwind romance when we met after meeting at church. I knew on our first date I was going to marry her. A short three weeks later, I purchased her engagement ring. She was the love of my life and I realized it immediately. I will never forget the way she looked when I walked into Baskin Robbins that first night. Yes, I know! Super fancy first date, right? I was such a big spender! Don't worry, I took it up a notch after the ice cream and took her to Starbucks. I don't even drink coffee. Honestly, it's amazing she agreed to go on a second date with me. Immediately following our first couple of dates, we started spending just about every free moment we had together. We very quickly knew our lives were going to be lived with one another and we were going to build a future side by side. I supported her whole heartedly in her profession as an attorney, and she equally supported me in the ministry and our church. Karla and I have never competed with one another. In fact, we see our roles as husband and wife as being meant to play an integral part of the other person reaching their highest level of development, success, and realization of God's purpose and calling for their life. Part of the roles we play in our marriage is we are very candid and forthright with each other, particularly when we think the other person is out of line. I have met many couples over the years who are afraid to speak their minds about their spouse to their spouse because they have previously received intense backlash when they have done so. I have never really understood that reaction. Why would you not want the person who loves you the most on this planet to be honest with you? If anyone should be able to look you in the face and respectfully tell you to change, it should be your husband or wife. One night, while we were still dating, we went to a fast-food restaurant in El Paso called Whataburger. Side note, it is the greatest, no question! We ordered our food at the drive through window, paid and proceeded to head to my house to eat. As we pulled out of the Whataburger parking lot, Karla began to challenge me about my attitude toward the staff at the restaurant. Without even noticing, I had apparently been quite rude to them. She informed me she was seeing a trend in how I treated people who I did not know personally. As I listened to her, I quickly and embarrassingly realized she was spot on in her assessment of my behavior. One statement she made to me was, "How can you be in the ministry and eventually be a pastor if you cannot even be nice to people?" OUCH!

John 7:38 — "He who believes in Me, as the Scripture has said, out of his heart will flow rivers of living water."

Karla changed my world that night and I am so glad she did. I spent a significant amount of time in the following months examining who I was and why I behaved the way I did. I was not achieving what Jesus stated in the above scripture – rivers of living water were not exactly flowing out of me. Why not? My life was good, not perfect, but good. I was healthy. I had a job within my career of choice. I had recently purchased my first home. I was in love with an amazing woman and about to get married. My parents were the pastors of a church where thousands of people loved me and were always incredibly kind to me. What did I have to complain about? The answer was, nothing! I had nothing to complain about and no reason to be a jerk, yet I was. The term "living water" that Jesus used in this verse means to be blessed abundantly by God, to be overflowing, to be fresh, to be fluid, and to be life-giving. I was all those things, minus the life-giving part. When I picture living water, I see a running stream or a flowing river – something that is a source of life, where nature flourishes and the circle of life operates in harmony. Living water perfectly describes itself. It produces life. As followers of Jesus, we are supposed to produce life. Our words and our actions should refresh, encourage and uplift those around us. We are not supposed to behave the way the world behaves. We should not be rude, mean, or demeaning to one another. We are to be living representatives of God's goodness and blessing to the world around us. Never forget that the god of the world system, Satan, has created this system of sin and deception to rob you of enjoying the life God has for you.

In my life, I have found that most Christians are on high alert to guard against the obvious sins of the world like greed, hatred, lust, adultery, pride or lying, but many completely underestimate what I believe is one of the most dangerous: negativity. Negativity is so damaging to your everyday life and your walk with God. It affects your attitude, your words, your mind and your soul. Negativity is pollution to your living water, and that is what I discovered was at the root of the issue within myself. I was ruled by negativity. By nature, a lot of humans are intensely negative. I was the consummate glass-half-empty guy. Honestly, I made pessimists look positive. I found fault in just about anything. I noticed every wrong detail of things without giving credit to how great something is. That was my nature, but does that make it right? Absolutely not. I had to change, and I did. Do you need to change too? Do you need to examine your outlook on life to find if it is truly in line with what God is doing for you? Is your perspective on the things taking place around you an actual representation of how blessed you are?

Proverbs 10:11 (Message) — *"The mouth of a good person is a deep, life-giving well, but the mouth of the wicked is a dark cave of abuse."*

This scripture shows a sharp contrast between two different types of people. The first is described as a good person who speaks positively and is depicted as a life-giving well. The second is wicked and abusive with their words. As a result, this person is portrayed as a dark cave of abuse. I have always enjoyed the imagery of this scripture. A well is something that is built on purpose, for a purpose, and that purpose is to sustain life. On the other hand, a cave is simply a result of nature. There is no intention behind it. A cave is completely ruled by nature. I picture a well, particularly in ancient times, as a gathering place and source of sustenance. I have no desire to spend time in caves. In fact, all I can think of when I think of a dark cave is there may be animals in there that can eat me. At best, I imagine there's creepy, crawly things like snakes and spiders. Maybe bats? No thank you.

It is interesting that the scripture paints this picture about humanity by basically drawing a line between an optimist and a pessimist. Which one are you? I used to be a pessimist. I am now an optimist. I determined to build my life on the good and not the bad. I decided to focus on what I can control, not on what I cannot. I grew very tired of always being the critic. I changed my mindset to one focused on what is right about God and not what was wrong with me. If I can do it, so can you. Like building a well, you can take control over your attitude and your outlook on life and completely reshape everything about yourself, including your happiness and even your influence on the happiness of people around you. Is your attitude solely driven by the elements — the news, your boss, traffic, etc.? Or is your attitude built intentionally on who God has made you to be, the promises of the abundant life Jesus came to give you, and His declaration of peace and goodwill toward all men? Are you a life-giving well, or a dark cave of abuse?

The best thing you can do is take your everyday life — your marriage, your health, your career, your hobbies — and give it to God. Embracing what God does for you is the greatest mental and emotional decision you can ever make. There is nothing negative about God. Everything about Him is good, and that goodness is directed toward you. He is the God of provision and supply. He is the God who is more than enough. The danger is you can become so well-adjusted to the negative culture of society that you conform to it without thought or resistance, becoming ruled by negativity, stress and worry. Going forward, focus your attention on Him and who He is for you. Build your life on the goodness of God, not the negativity of the world. If you are going to conform to anything, conform to the thinking and ways of God. His thoughts are better than the world's thoughts. His ways are better than your ways. And His results are the results you want! His results produce a life of peace, fulfillment and satisfaction. There is no other way like God's way. Life will never be perfect on earth, but there really is so much good. You are blessed. The danger is to not recognize it and only notice what is wrong.

Please understand that negativity is completely contrary to godliness and living the way Jesus wants you to live. The Bible says God has given you a living hope through Jesus, who is the hope of humanity. A living hope is to have a positive expectation of good for your future in every season and aspect of your life. If you are ruled by negativity though, your mind will be dominated by worry and anxiety, not hope. Negativity always expects the worst thing to happen.

"Nothing good ever happens for us."

"Everyone is against me."

"What's the use in trying anyway?"

"Why even bother anymore?"

We have all uttered phrases like this to make ourselves feel better during situations that did not work out well, but the reality is these statements are false. That negativity is causing you to make broad generalizations about life and circumstance, resulting in a defeated mentality. Proverbs 12:25 (NIV) says, *"Anxiety weighs down the heart, but a kind word cheers it up."* A kind word is a positive word. Negativity and anxiety go hand in hand. In fact, negativity is the starting point to anxiety, and anxiety leads to worry and depression. Makes perfect sense, doesn't it? That is why you must stand against and root out negativity from having dominion over your thoughts, words, attitude and expectation. The compound effect of unbridled negativity produces a self-fulfilled prophecy of hopelessness and ultimate failure. Failure is the enemy's goal. He knows he cannot control you. He is aware of the fact he cannot rule you. He understands fully he has no power and authority over your life. There is nothing Satan can do to change the course of victory Jesus has given you – unless you decide to defeat yourself. That is why negativity is so prevalent in our world today.

215

1 John 5:4 — *"And this is the victory that has overcome the world- our faith."*

Hebrews 10:38 — *"Now the just shall live by faith."*

Hebrews 11:1 — *"Now faith is the substance of things hoped for, the evidence of things not seen."*

Faith is the power God has given to all those who believe in Him to overcome the world system. We are to live by faith. Our manner of life is to be built on faith. Faith is what you believe and speak. If your expectation is a negative one, your faith will be averse to the peace and provision God is trying to empower your life with.

As you now realize hope is the mentality God wants you to allow to rule your soul, you should also see that hope and faith are divinely connected. Faith brings to life what you are hoping for. If you lose hope in life, you ultimately lose faith. Without hope, faith has nothing to do; therefore, exposing the purpose behind the negative onslaught life brings toward you. Satan simply wants to discourage you into relinquishing your living hope, so you walk by fear and not by faith. Negativity is the antithesis of hope. When you walk by fear, you are accepting defeat. He cannot defeat you unless you consciously, or more likely subconsciously, defeat yourself by having the wrong expectation. Hope is your lifeline to the goodness of God. Negativity convinces you to talk yourself out of believing that you are strong, capable, wise and free, able to overcome the challenges of life.

216

The nation of Israel under the leadership of Moses is a great example of what I am talking about. Moses, by the power of God, had delivered the entire nation from captivity in Egypt. He led them through the desert to the land God promised to give them. There were to be twelve different allotments of land distributed to the tribes of the nation upon inhabiting the land. God had promised to give them victory over the people of the incredible land that flowed with milk and honey. In the literal text of the Bible, the promised land is described as a land that promotes health, welfare and prosperity. Sound familiar? Upon their arrival at the border of the promised land, Moses chose one man from each tribe to go spy the land and bring back a report of what was going on behind the walls.

Here is the account of the report the spies brought back to Moses and their people:

Numbers 13:25-33 — *"And they returned from spying out the land after forty days. Now they departed and came back to Moses and Aaron and all the congregation of the children of Israel in the Wilderness of Paran, at Kadesh; they brought back word to them and to all the congregation, and showed them the fruit of the land. Then they told him and said: "We went to the land where you sent us. It truly flows with milk and honey, and this is its fruit. Nevertheless, the people who dwell in the land are strong; the cities are fortified and very large; moreover, we saw the descendants of Anak there. The Amalekites dwell in the land of the South; the Hittites, the Jebusites, and the Amorites dwell in the mountains; and the Canaanites dwell by the sea and along the banks of the Jordan." Then Caleb quieted the people before Moses, and said, "Let us go up at once and take possession, for we are well able to overcome it." But the men who had gone up with him said, "We are not able to go up against the people, for they are stronger than we." And they gave the children of Israel a bad report of the land which they had spied out, saying, "The land through which we have gone as spies is a land that devours its inhabitants, and all the people whom we saw in it are men of great stature. There we saw the giants (the descendants of Anak came from the giants); and we were like grasshoppers in our own sight, and so we were in their sight."*

This is truly one of the saddest stories recorded in the Bible. The mighty nation of Israel is standing at the doorstep of their new home. God has delivered them from captivity in Egypt. These are the same men and women that witnessed God split the Red Sea to free them from being pursued by the tyrannical ruler named Pharaoh. He has kept them safe from harm, provided food, water, heating and cooling as He led them through desert. The entire nation is fully aware and has born firsthand witness to God's mighty power and care for them. They are also completely up to speed on the plan and the promise God made to them generations before they were even born. The time is at hand. Their destiny is ready to be realized. The God of the universe is on their side. All they must do is take the land – and they do not do it. They quite literally talk themselves out of seeing their dreams come true. Not because they were unable. Not because defeat was imminent. Not because the walls were too fortified or the inhabitants too powerful. None of those reasons were true. They did not enter the promised land solely due to the damaging power and influence negativity was given within their camps. An entire generation chose to go back into the wilderness to die instead of inhabiting the land God had promised them. Let's take a look at what happened, so you can be on guard against the same thing happening to you.

■ Negativity Blurs
1 Your Vision

Verse 27-28 — *"We went to the land where you sent us. It truly flows with milk and honey, and this is its fruit. Nevertheless, the people who dwell in the land are strong; the cities are fortified and very large."*

Upon returning to their camps after spying the land, the twelve men reported to Moses and their leadership that the land is truly what God said it would be – it flowed with milk and honey. Immediately though, their tone changed. "Nevertheless," they said as they went on to overwhelm their countrymen with how strong the inhabitants were and how large the cities were. God had never failed them, and He had no intention of suddenly doing so in this moment. Negativity caused these people to lose sight of the fact that God's promise was true and instead focus on the challenge standing in their way. In every area of your life, you can find negative things if you are looking for them. There is plenty of it to go around in our imperfect world, but you do not have to allow it to stop you. Why don't you start trying to focus on the opportunities that lie beyond overcoming challenge and obstacle, instead of being overwhelmed by it? Negativity clouds your vision to only see what is wrong and bad while ignoring what is right and good. The ruling pattern of your mind is what will determine what you see in life. If your mind is negative, you will see all the bad. If your mind is positive, you will see all the good. Here is a reality of life: you are ruled mentally and emotionally by what you see. If you see life like a dark cave of defeat, that is exactly how you will live. If you begin to reject being overcome by negativity, you will begin to see life like a living well and your mind will be filled with gratitude, joy and peace. Do not allow the enemy to rob you of seeing just how blessed you truly are. Do not talk yourself out of the greatness of God that He put in your heart simply because greatness is often difficult to achieve. Do not miss out on a fulfilled promise or a realized dream because you allowed a couple of wrongs to overrule the rights.

218

2 Negativity is a Liar

Verse 32 — *"And they gave the children of Israel a bad report of the land which they had spied out, saying, "The land through which we have gone as spies is a land that devours its inhabitants, and all the people whom we saw in it are men of great stature."*

What a contradiction in this one scripture. They have previously stated that the land flows with milk and honey and now they give a bad report. Then they say that the land "devours its inhabitants" but go on to describe the giants of the land. How can that be? Their statements do not make any sense at all. Clearly, the land does not devour its inhabitants if the inhabitants are giants and you are now stating that you cannot overtake them. That is the effect unbridled negativity has in your mind. It causes you to believe contradictions and tell yourself a lie. This is the genesis of getting you to live a defeated life. That is exactly what happened to the nation of Israel and it can happen to you if you do not control negativity within yourself. You must win the battle of the mind! There will always be reasons not to take a leap of faith. You can always talk yourself out of doing something amazing. If you talk to enough people, someone will eventually give you a contradiction to hope and faith that will attempt to justify inaction. If you search for excuses, you will find them. **You can have excuses, or you can have results, but you cannot have both.** Please do not believe the lie. If God said He will do something, He is faithful to do it. If God said you can overcome depression, then you can be overcome depression. If God inspired you to go back to school, go get yourself registered. There will always be "why nots" in life. Sometimes you just have to go for it. Do not accept the contradiction to the truth. Do not allow hope to be turned into hopelessness, faith into fear, and peace into torment.

3 Negativity Spreads and Attracts

The nation of Israel consisted of over three million people at the time of this incredible story. Think about this for a moment:

ten men caused three million to give up on their destiny. What a tragedy. I view negativity like water. It finds the path of least resistance and flows wherever possible until controlled. Like attracts like. Birds of a feather flock together. Negativity spreads like a wildfire and tries to destroy everything in its path. I read a meme one time online that said, "Be careful what you say to a negative person, they've got a problem for every solution." In my years of leadership, I have found this statement to be incredibly true. I have also noticed over time that negative people tend to hang around other negative people, until they turn their negativity on each other of course. The nation of Israel did this. They turned on the spies, turned on Moses and even turned on God. You simply cannot underestimate the damning force negativity becomes when it goes unchecked.

Proverbs 13:20 (Message) — *"Become wise by walking with the wise; hang out with fools and watch your life fall to pieces."*

At this point, I think you can agree with me that negativity is foolish, and hope is wise. Who are you hanging out with? Whose voice are you allowing to speak into your life? Who are you listening to? Are the people in your life building you up or tearing you down? Are they encouraging you or discouraging you? Are they filling you with hope or despair? Do the people you spend the most time with lead to wells of life or dark caves of abuse? Life can be hard. There are plenty of things to be stressed over and worry about. The last thing you need is people who only point out what you do not have, everything you have done wrong, or how horrible things are. You need to find some people in your life like Caleb and Joshua in the nation of Israel. After the bad report was given by the ten spies, Caleb spoke up and said, "Let us go up at once and take possession, for we are well able to overcome it." Caleb saw exactly the same challenges the other spies saw, but he did not allow himself to be ruled them. In fact, forty years later, he and Joshua would lead the nation of Israel to victory and possess the promised land. Find yourself people of hope and faith to speak into your life. At a minimum, you be that person for people in your life.

220

4 Negativity Diminishes Your Confidence

Verse 33 — *"There we saw the giants (the descendants of Anak came from the giants); and we were like grasshoppers in our own sight, and so we were in their sight."*

God's chosen people, whom He had delivered and led to this moment, could not see themselves or their God for who they were and what He was going to do. All they saw was the size of the giants in the land, and they became "like grasshoppers" in their own minds. If you are not mindful of negativity and determined to confront and reject it, it will unleash an all-out assault on your confidence until you are living a defeated life, crushed by opposition, disappointment and failure. It accomplishes this goal by attacking your insecurities.

> "I'm not smart enough."
> "I'm not old/young enough."
> "I'm not the right person."
> "I don't deserve to be happy."

Negativity will always try to keep you in the dark cave, but it ultimately becomes self-abuse that leads to a self-fulfilling prophecy of defeat. Stand firm today on hope. Let hope anchor your soul. Grab onto hope with both hands and never let go. No matter what you face, no matter how you feel, no matter where you are, always remind yourself to have a positive expectation of good for your future.

Romans 15:13 — *"Now may the God of hope fill you with all joy and peace in believing, that you may abound in hope by the power of the Holy Spirit."*

Hope and peace go hand-in-hand in life. Where there is hope, there will be peace. Jeremiah 29:11 says that the thoughts of God toward you are full of peace and His plans are to give you a future and a hope. How can you not have hope when you understand that the God of hope and peace has declared health, welfare, prosperity and all sorts of good things over your life? The greatest asset you possess to overcome the assault on your confidence and the unrelenting pressure to live according to your insecurities and doubts is hope. Hope is what carries you through the good times and the challenging ones. If you are going to believe in anything for the rest of your life, believe in hope. Stand firm in having a positive expectation. Pay attention to the good that is in your life. Remember how far you have come and the victories you have had in the past. Walk confidently, regardless of situation and circumstance, knowing God is always on your side. Live in hope.

◼ Negativity Steals
5 Your Promise

Numbers 14:1-3 — *"So all the congregation lifted up their voices and cried, and the people wept that night. And all the children of Israel complained against Moses and Aaron, and the whole congregation said to them, 'If only we had died in the land of Egypt! Or if only we had died in this wilderness! Why has the Lord brought us to this land to fall by the sword, that our wives and children should become victims? Would it not be better for us to return to Egypt?'"*

An entire generation of people never got to see their promise become a reality, not because the promise was not ready to be fulfilled, but rather, because they allowed negativity to become hopelessness. Their hopelessness produced a despair that talked them out of faith and into fear. The enemy uses negativity to attack your mind, skew your point of view, and influence you into living a life of defeat and victimization. Do not be like the nation of Israel and live an "if only" life. God does not bring you opportunities to then abandon you as you pursue maximizing them. God is not man. He does not lie, and He does not fail. To the nation of Israel's credit, they learned from their mistake. As the story goes, they spent forty more years wandering the wilderness before their children would return to the land God had promised them. Upon doing so, Joshua and Caleb immediately lead the people to victory. That tells me that the parents who did not go into the land taught their children to avoid making the same mistake they had made. They clearly raised the next generation to pursue their dreams and trust God to fulfill His Word in their lives. That should encourage you as you read it. If they could change, so can you. Maybe you have been in a dark cave of abuse in the past, but now you can choose to be a well of life. Maybe you were a pessimist who found fault in everything, but now you can be an optimist and start seeing the good in life. Stop being ruled by what is wrong and start being encouraged by what is right. Focus on who you are with God and He will lead you to an amazing life of joy, hope and peace.

2 Corinthians 1:20 — *"For all the promises of God in Him are yes, and in Him amen, to the glory of God through us."*

God sealed His promises, all of which make your life better, with a great yes and a wonderful amen when Jesus rose from the grave over two thousand years ago. You have been called unto peace by the God of peace Himself, and there is nothing anyone can do to change this amazing reality. All you must do is allow yourself to understand the attack the enemy brings against you, and consequently overcome it as you realize your victory. You are not powerless in this life. You are a child of God. You are strong. You are able. You are filled with hope. You walk by faith, and you will live in peace.

223

Joy and Happiness

THE MISSING PEACE

Joy and Happiness

Humor me for a moment and close your eyes. I want you to picture your happy place. Maybe it is sitting on a beach watching the tide roll in under the backdrop of a beautiful sunset. It might be cozied up in your favorite chair by the fireplace with a great novel after the kids have fallen asleep. It could be just the opposite, and your happy place is a room filled with the people you love the most celebrating a birthday or holiday together sharing food, memories and laughter. Happiness is something every person longs for. We read books about it, we scan through magazines that give us tips to find it, we scroll through social media comparing our lives to other people's thinking we would be happy if we had what they have, and we make purchases hoping certain material goods will bring it to us. Everyone wants to be happy, yet too often happiness is not what we should be pursuing. Happiness is fickle and circumstantial and only results in bursts of satisfaction and fulfillment. It is entirely based on situations or things going precisely as planned. What we should be pursuing is joy. Joy is everything happiness is not.

Joy is an emotion acquired by the anticipation, acquisition, or even the expectation of something great or wonderful taking place. Where happiness is temporary and subject to external conditions, joy is permanent, steady and determined by a state of mind and disposition. Joy can even remain during the most challenging of times in your life. **You can live in a state of joy amid circumstances that have little or no happiness.** The Bible speaks of Jesus enduring the cross with great joy in His heart. How is that possible? It is because joy is not determined by what is happening to you, it is determined by what is happening in you. This is possible because even in pain, you can live knowing that better days are ahead of you. Joy comes from understanding the God of peace has a hope and a future for you. Joy is an emotion set on the prospect that God is always good, He never forsakes you, and He is working on your behalf to create for you a great future. Romans 12:12 says to be joyful in hope. Romans 15:13 shows you the God of hope will fill you with joy and peace as you trust in Him. James 1:2 even says to consider it a joy when you face trials and challenges. You can only have joy during tribulation if you know God has given you the victory and you are going to overcome whatever obstacle is in your life at that moment. And that is the reality of every person who serves God. Every believer in Jesus can live with a great expectation that the God of peace is pouring out His blessing and favor on their lives.

Galatians 5:22-23 — *"But the fruit of the Spirit is love, joy, peace, longsuffering, kindness, goodness, faithfulness, gentleness, self-control. Against such there is no law."*

Romans 14:17 — *"For the kingdom of God is not eating and drinking, but righteousness and peace and joy in the Holy Spirit."*

226

Happiness is a temporary emotion that can be felt. Joy is not an emotion that is acquired, it is a gift from God that can be possessed permanently. The Bible says all God's children are joint heirs to His promises. You are the beneficiary of a divine inheritance from the Lord, and joy is part of the inheritance you receive for being in God's family. Joy is a state of mind and a setting within your heart that is received through the hope and peace of God; but, it is attained by choice. You can receive this amazing gift by determining within yourself that it is not anyone else's responsibility to make you happy. You can live in a state of joy by refusing to be daunted by the difficulties life will inevitably bring your way. Your soul can be joyful knowing God is always on your side and He never fails. Joy is not defined by a location, a moment in time, people or possessions. Happiness is defined by those things. **Joy is defined by you.** It is found in who you truly are as a loved and forgiven child of God, living in the reality of the calling of peace on your life. You do not have to be wealthy to have joy. You do not have to have the perfect family to have joy. You do not have to drive an expensive car to have joy. All you need to do is rest in the truth of who God is for you and what His plan for your life is.

Nehemiah 8:10 — *"Do not sorrow, for the joy of the Lord is your strength."*

After reading this book and having your eyes opened to all that God has, all that He is, and all that He will do for you, I truly encourage you to choose joy as the posture of your life. Yes, it is up to you to choose joy. No one can choose it for you. In fact, living a joyful life starts with you deciding to choose joy. We all know that every choice has a consequence, good or bad. For every action, there is a reaction. The beauty of choosing joy is that the consequence is strength. That is why the enemy tries so hard to pilfer it from your life. Like every other gift from God, Satan will always try to diminish its effect, minimize its power, and steal its benefit from your life. Satan does not want you to live with strength. The last thing he wants to see is millions of bold, confident, and faith-filled believers determined to overcome the world system of negativity, cynicism and darkness at any cost. He wants you to think you are weak, that you are a lost cause. He wants you to convince yourself you are far too removed from the possibilities of joy and happiness. You do not have to play his foolish games any longer. You are now empowered to redefine your life, to guard your heart and discipline your mind into a place of peace, hope and joy. Proverbs 17:22 says, *"A merry heart does good, like medicine, but a broken spirit dries the bones."* The incredible truth about joy is it really does affect you on multiple levels. Joy has been linked to a reduction of stress, anxiety and even physical and mental ailments. With that said, please understand that the acquisition of joy is a continual process you must attend to, fight for, and protect as you move forward in life, or you will live with a broken spirit as stated in Proverbs.

227

PROVERBS 17:22

"A merry heart does good, like medicine, but a broken spirit dries the bones."

Broken is no way to live, and you do not have to. If you are anything like me, your life is inundated with people and attitudes that try to impede your joy. They are contradictions intentionally designed to knock you off course. Make no mistake, there are countless forces trying to influence you constantly, many of which are negative. You, and only you, are in absolute control of your attitude.

Your attitude. Your choice.

■ Faithfulness
1 Over Entitlement

Entitlement is a joy crusher. Unfortunately, it appears that more and more of our society is living with an entitled spirit, but it is not bringing them the fulfillment they crave so deeply. Entitlement is selfish and presumptive. It is the belief that one is inherently deserving of privileges or special treatment. Entitlement will cause you to gripe about what you do not have. Instead, be inspired to work for it, set goals to achieve it, and move toward fulfillment. Entitlement says, "I deserve what is not mine. I deserve what I did not earn." This type of attitude rarely makes dreams come true. Entitlement has recently become more and more prevalent, but it is not how society actually functions. Even when entitlement gets you what you want, there will rarely be joy associated with it because you know you did not earn it. That type of disposition only leads to more entitlement, not satisfaction.

Matthew 25:23 — *"You have been faithful over a few things, I will make you ruler over many things. Enter into the joy of your Lord."*

Rarely in life are opportunities or great experiences presented to you in a perfect way, like a Christmas present with a red bow on it. Life is not perfect. Greatness is never easy. Success is complicated, at times messy, and usually quite challenging. Most great opportunities test you and require you to focus and be resilient over even the smallest details, but that is where joy and satisfaction comes. There is nothing more fulfilling than knowing you did something fantastic while persevering through the obstacles that came your way. Faithfulness is the belief that one earns what they work for and receives what they rightly deserved. Great marriages are built by being kind and loving to each other every day. You get a promotion or raise at work because you show up on time and go above and beyond expectations. You get in shape by consistently eating healthy and exercising. Jesus, in the scripture above, tied faithfulness to increase and joy. That is obvious, right? Of course, joy comes as you succeed in life. The beautiful truth here is anyone can be faithful. It is not a talent you are born with; it is a choice of character you decide on. Anyone can choose to be reliable, honest, trustworthy, loyal and constant in the various roles they play in life. When you choose faithfulness, you choose growth, advancement, promotion and joy. When you choose entitlement, you choose frustration, disappointment and emptiness.

◼ Celebrating Over
2 Complaining

It is astounding how much people complain about in life. I have a feeling we are all guilty of it too. I'm willing to admit I have a natural tendency to complain. We complain at home, at work, online, while out and about, and even politically. Quite often, we complain about anything else we can find there to be imperfections. Therein lies the problem. If you want to complain, you will have plenty to complain about. But does it do you any good mentally or emotionally? Of course not. Complaining does nothing but sap your joy and suck the life out of potentially good things. Complaining demeans people's effort and devalues their contributions. It is so easy to gripe and whine. It takes no talent or ability to point out problems and express your dissatisfaction about something or someone. The real talent rests in those who look beyond people's faults to find solutions to the problems or offer alternatives to avoid the many nuisances that arise in life. The greatest and most successful leaders are not stopped by wrongs, they are driven to find what is right. There is no greater satisfaction to be found than in righting a wrong.

PHILIPPIANS 4:4

"Rejoice in the Lord always. Again I will say rejoice!"

Psalms 32:11 — *"Be glad in the Lord and rejoice, you righteous; and shout for joy, all you upright in heart!"*

The antonyms in the dictionary for complaining are celebrating and rejoicing. As much as there is to complain about in life, there is far more to celebrate and rejoice about. The earth is full of good things and the goodness of God. The posture of your heart should be to rejoice in the blessing God has bestowed upon your life. The very fact that He loves you unconditionally and has promised you an eternity in Heaven living without sin, sadness, pain or weeping is enough to glorify and honor Him every day for the rest of your time on the earth. But this posture of celebration should not just be pointed toward God. We should celebrate people. We should applaud great accomplishments. We should honor effort, sacrifice and hard work. Integrity, diligence and commitment should still be rewarded in our culture. We should look for and find the good in life. Yes, fix what is wrong. Don't ignore it. Address the mistakes that are made, but you do not have to lose your joy over them. Nobody is perfect, including you. Let me ask you a question. Who do you want to spend time with: the person who complains about everything you do wrong, or the person who celebrates your endeavors and accomplishments? The answer is obvious of course. Now I challenge you to become that person. The Bible says to rejoice when others rejoice and weep when others weep. Be glad and shout for joy! That is a great way to live.

◼ Gratitude Over
3 Criticism

Critical thinking is one of the greatest assets a person can have. Many great leaders of society, businesses and sports teams are critical thinkers. They are the ones who can critique something in order to improve upon its performance or efficiency. As valuable as critical thinking is, a critical spirit is detrimental in equal measure. A critical spirit does not critique to improve. A critical spirit critiques to tear down, hurt or debase others. It is not about improving the quality of someone or something; rather, it is about projecting cruel words and behavior toward others.

Luke 6:37-38 (Message) — *"Don't pick on people, jump on their failures, criticize their faults—unless, of course, you want the same treatment. Don't condemn those who are down; that hardness can boomerang. Be easy on people; you'll find life a lot easier. Give away your life; you'll find life given back, but not merely given back—given back with bonus and blessing. Giving, not getting, is the way. Generosity begets generosity."*

As a pastor, I am criticized constantly. If I am being completely honest, it's not very fun. Rarely is it informed, helpful or filled with any sort of empathy or benefit of the doubt. It is usually ignorant, unkind words projected at someone they know little about. It is easy to criticize a movie after you have watched it to its conclusion, but have you ever made a movie? It is easy to criticize your favorite quarterback after throwing an interception, but have you played professional sports? It is easy to criticize a meal at a restaurant, but are you a chef? Take it easy on people. Encourage them, help them, strengthen them and try to empower people to do great things. Don't just stand on the sidelines of the game of life and point out everyone's faults. There is no skill in that, and there is definitely not any joy. Get in the game. Try your best, face your fears, fall and get back up, and maybe – just maybe – you will do something amazing. Take it easy on people. We have enough people in society trying to tear people apart. Give people the benefit of the doubt when things they produce are not perfect. Try to exercise some empathy and compassion. And like the above scripture says, do not forget you reap what you sow.

231

The spirit of criticism finds no benefit to celebration, creativity or gratitude. Gratitude starves this spirit. 1 Thessalonians 5:18 says, *"In everything give thanks."* In case this is not clear enough, everything means everything. The good times, the bad times, the challenging times, the lonely times, the wonderful times, and every other time you encounter, give thanks. No matter what is going on in your life, there is far more to be grateful for than there is to be upset about. A spirit of gratitude and thankfulness brings so much joy to your own heart and to those around you. Gratitude forces you to see the good in people. Gratitude inspires kind and encouraging words and actions. There is simply no substitute for thankfulness in your soul. Here is a challenge for you: right now, I want you to write down five things you are grateful for. Now, I want you to repeat that exercise every day for the next week. At the end of the week, you will have thirty-five things to find joy in. Every time you feel your critical spirit trying to overcome your soul, find five new things to be grateful for.

◼ Forgiveness Over
4 Bitterness

Forgiveness is freedom, plain and simple. If you want to live without joy and happiness in your life, hang on to all the wrongs, hurts and disappointments people have done to you in the past. The poverty that unforgiveness brings into your heart and mind is incomprehensible when left unchecked. Living in the past will never allow you to get where God wants you to go in the future. It is time to forget the pain of the past and move forward with freedom in your soul, into a joy-filled future. Too often, people do not want to forgive those who wronged them because they feel like they are vindicating, justifying or freeing those people from what they did. That is a lie of the enemy. Forgiveness is not about freeing the person who wronged you. Forgiveness is about freeing yourself. Haven't they hurt you enough? Haven't you cried enough tears over someone who broke your heart or betrayed you? Unforgiveness gives people who do not have your best interest in mind power and authority over your joy and happiness. It is time to take that power back. Stop letting people who clearly do not or did not love you enough to treat you with the appropriate levels of respect, decency and kindness have rule over your joy.

Hebrews 12:15 — *"Looking carefully lest anyone fall short of the grace of God; lest any root of bitterness springing up cause trouble, and by this many become defiled."*

Unforgiveness is a breeding ground for bitterness. Have you ever met someone who is so bitter about issues from the past that they cannot enjoy the good that is happening to them in the present? I think we all have. They are hard-hearted, angry, grumpy and cynical. **Bitterness is like quicksand. The more you struggle with**

it, the more it pulls you down. That is why the above scripture in Hebrews calls it the "root of bitterness." If you do not kill the root, it will spread throughout every area of your life. I have seen people have a bad experience in their career, become bitter about it, and consequently destroy their marriage. Sure enough, they then become bitter toward relationships, and so on and so forth. Bitterness enables the pain of the past to steal the joy of the present. You will never possess the fullness of joy God wants you to have with unforgiveness in your heart. It is time to forgive. Forgive those who have wronged you. Forgive those who have disappointed you. Forgive those who have said horrible things about you. Forgive those who have betrayed your trust. Forgive those who lied about you. Lastly, it is time to forgive yourself as well. Yes, you have made mistakes, maybe terrible ones. God has forgiven you. Why don't you do the same? You have punished yourself enough about what happened. As the chapters of this book come to a conclusion, be free from the prison of unforgiveness and the root of bitterness.

■ Giving Over
5 Receiving   233

The Bible says it is truly more blessed to give than to receive, and I believe that with all my heart. One of the greatest joys of being of father of two young kids is watching them open their Christmas presents. The anticipation, the excitement, and the utter happiness they express as they tear the wrapping paper off to see what is inside is pure joy. I love every second of it. Sure, getting presents is great, but there is nothing that brings me more delight than giving them to the people I love. Large parts of our society have become increasingly selfish as of late. "What's in it for me? What's good for me? What's best for me?" That sounds like the right attitude, but research has proven that people who think that way are far less happy than those who look to find the best for themselves **and** for those around them. *"Give away your life;"* Luke 6:38 (The Message) says, *"you'll find life given back, but not merely given back—given back with bonus and blessing. Giving, not getting, is the way. Generosity begets generosity."* There is enough of God's peace and blessing for everyone to enjoy. Other people's success

"Bitterness is like quicksand. The more you struggle with it, the more it pulls you down."

does not mean you cannot be successful. Other people's happiness does not mean you cannot be happy. If anything, you should be inspired by the success and happiness of people around you. True joy is found in experiencing it with others. Make no mistake, joy is contagious and giving is the way to spread it.

Proverbs 11:24-25 (Message) — *"The world of the generous gets larger and larger; the world of the stingy gets smaller and smaller. The one who blesses others is abundantly blessed; those who help others are helped."*

A simple fact of life is that generosity begets generosity, kindness begets kindness, helps begets help, peace begets peace, and joy begets joy. The amazing reality is that to bless someone else, it means you have already been blessed. You cannot give what you do not have. To give means you have already received, and received at a level that is more than enough for what you needed in the first place. In your overflow, God empowers you to spread joy, kindness, love, forgiveness and hope. Incredibly, God also values your giving, and He rewards it. Go live a generous life and you will never lack joy in your heart. Truly, generosity makes the world go round.

Isaiah 55:11-12 - *"So shall My word be that goes forth from My mouth; it shall not return to Me void, but it shall accomplish what I please, and it shall prosper in the thing for which I sent it. For you shall go out with joy, and be led out with peace."*

The entirety of this book is founded upon Godly principles and His Word. The reason for this is because His Word is the Word of Peace. His Word is what He watches over to perform and bring to fruition in your life. His Word inspires joy and leads you to tranquility for your heart and mind. It allows you to understand you live in favor with God, walking in the hope of health, welfare, prosperity, and all kinds of good things happening now, and in your future, because the God of all blessing is working on your behalf. God's Word cannot be ignored, and it never returns to Him void. What He says becomes reality. He spoke peace and goodwill over you, and there is nothing anyone can do to change it. No matter what you may have been through, no matter what you may be facing right now, this is God's plan, desire and will for you. Be filled with joy in this moment, knowing that your best days are ahead of you. Good things are happening!

Trust the Process

Trust the Process

Mark 4:26-29 (Message) — *"Then Jesus said, 'God's kingdom is like seed thrown on a field by a man who then goes to bed and forgets about it. The seed sprouts and grows—he has no idea how it happens. The earth does it all without his help: first a green stem of grass, then a bud, then the ripened grain. When the grain is fully formed, he reaps—harvest time!'"*

The scriptures you just read highlight a very important truth of every person's reality here on this beautiful planet. The issue is we do not always acknowledge or desire to function within this truth. But whether we like or not, agree with it or not, desire it or not, just about everything in life is defined and ruled by process. If we could have it our way, we would often skip the details and go straight to the end result, but that is just not how God's system works. You do not get in great physical shape by showing up to the gym one time. You do not build up the endurance to run a marathon by going for a short jog every once in a while. You do not build, or rebuild, a happy and strong marriage by only being nice to one another sparingly. Even our education system is a process. You start in kindergarten and advance annually to new levels of progression and achievement as you grow mentally and physically. You do not take Algebra 1 and graduate to Advanced Calculus immediately. As Jesus pointed out, the Kingdom of Heaven is like a seed being sown. You plant the seed and trust the process of nature to turn the seed into a harvest. It is humanly impossible to turn a seed into a harvest overnight. My goal in authoring this book was to lay out a step-by-step process for anyone missing peace. By reading, understanding and applying the steps in this process, you will allow the divine promises of God to do exactly what they do – produce change and good!

This book has sown the seed of truth into your heart and mind by illuminating the reality of God's declaration of peace over your life. You now know you can be free, and the peace that has been absent from your life for far too long can now be present. At this point, you just need to trust the process. Does it always happen overnight? Not necessarily. That can be a problem if you allow it to be. The enemy will try to discourage you and tell you what you have read does not work, or that it only works for certain people. He will try to convince you that you are a lost cause, but **you are not.** You must fight the instant gratification frustration that is so easy to succumb to. I have shared throughout these chapters some of the challenges and struggles I overcame myself. I wish I could tell you that I now live every day of my life without worry or anxiety. If I said that, I would be lying to you. I still have to trust the process God gave me to maintain my peace. The challenge, though, is the desire for instant gratification. Let's tell the truth: this is, in large part, the world we live in. News stories are updated online minute by minute. Order groceries on a delivery app and they are at your doorstep within hours. We do not even have to wonder about things anymore. We just Google it and within seconds we have all the information we will ever need to answer our questions. When I was growing up, you had to go to a public library or read an encyclopedia. You do not even have to wait for your favorite song to come on the radio anymore like I did when I was younger. Now, you just pull it up on your streaming service and listen to what you want on demand. If a website does not load immediately, do you wait? If you are anything like me, you just move on to the next one. Instant gratification can be very discouraging if you allow it to be. The seed has been sown, now you can water it, shine some light on it, and let it grow. After you conclude this book, will you have times when you need to guard your heart? Of course, you will. Will you have moments when your mind tries to run wild on you to convince you the world is caving in and you will never climb out from under it? Of course, you will. Will the memories of the mistakes and the hurt from the past try to creep up with shame, regret and condemnation, weighing you down and stealing your joy? Yes, absolutely these things will all happen, but unlike in the past, you now know how to guard your heart and discipline your mind so your peace cannot go missing once again. Please do not be discouraged if you still struggle mentally or emotionally from time to time. Remember, you must take a stand for your freedom, while also keeping in mind that the peace of God is there for the taking. It is your divine calling from God. Now, just trust the process.

Learning to Be Content

Philippians 4:4-13 — *"Rejoice in the Lord always. Again I will say, rejoice! Let your gentleness be known to all men. The Lord is at hand. Be anxious for nothing, but in everything by prayer and supplication, with thanksgiving, let your requests be made known to God; and the peace of God, which surpasses all understanding, will guard your hearts and minds through Christ Jesus. Finally, brethren, whatever things are true, whatever things are noble, whatever things are just, whatever things are pure, whatever things are lovely, whatever things are of good report, if there is any virtue and if there is anything praiseworthy—meditate on these things. The things which you learned and received and heard and saw in me, these do, and the God of peace will be with you. But I rejoiced in the Lord greatly that now at last your care for me has flourished again; though you surely did care, but you lacked opportunity. Not that I speak in regard to need, for I have learned in whatever state I am, to be content: I know how to be abased, and I know how to abound. Everywhere and in all things I have learned both to be full and to be hungry, both to abound and to suffer need. I can do all things through Christ who strengthens me."*

239

As we have throughout this book, let's look one last time at the Apostle Paul's great writing. After he reveals the process of allowing the peace of God to protect our hearts and minds beyond human comprehension, he reveals another great truth. *"For I have learned in whatever state I am, to be content"* (Philippians 4:11). The ultimate goal of life is to be able to be content no matter what is going on in front of us. To be content is to have peace of mind while maintaining mental and emotional satisfaction. Whether you are in a season of challenge or one of ease, whether you are overflowing in financial provision or barely getting by, whether life is on your desired path or has taken a detour, you can learn to be content. It is interesting Paul said he *learned* to be content. That means it did not come naturally to him. It was a process he trusted and worked into his life as an Apostle. He had to decide to focus on the right things and find joy in the right places. Too often, people search for peace and satisfaction in all the wrong places, and the results are not ones they are happy with. But you have now learned, and will continue to learn, to maintain your peace and joy. Too often, people grow learning to be discontent rather than content. They do not like where they are, what they are doing, and who they have become. People are often accustomed to allowing the temperament of their surroundings to have far too much control over their happiness. Habits of overreacting, panicking, stressing and worrying over what people are saying, what we have or do not have, or what took place in the past have disrupted our souls into a place of dissatisfaction and frustration. The beauty of Paul's statement here is that if you can learn something, you can also unlearn it – or you can choose to learn something new. You may have had one process of doing things; now, you can establish a new one. Discontentment is destitution to your soul, and it is opposed to the will of God for your life. The final statement written in the above scripture states, *"I can do all things through Christ who strengthens me"* (v. 13). Yes, with God on your side and your promise of peace, you can do all things, including learning how to be content and living a peace-filled life.

I pray you will settle within yourself that you are a person of peace who is in complete control over your heart and mind. Even during difficulties and trials, you can maintain your mind's tranquility because you know God wants the best for you. Contentment is not found in the circumstance; it is found within your heart and mind through Jesus Christ. The peace of God is the foundational source of being content. Please understand, being content does not mean you have to accept difficulties as the reality for your future; but on the contrary, being content says your soul will not be overwhelmed by this challenge. Being content says you will keep your faith and trust God is going to get you through this and take you to something better. Being content is not settling for less than God has planned for you. Being content is not becoming indifferent about life so you just do not feel anything anymore and wind up living a life of uselessness. Being content is not quitting or resigning to fate with a "whatever happens will happen" attitude. Being content is simply being in command of your joy, and not being controlled by outside forces. You learn to be content as you realize Jesus is more than enough for you, His promises are true, and He wants you to be well supplied. Lack, in any area, is not the destiny of God's children – yourself included. Understanding this truth for your life will always settle your heart and mind. When you live content that Christ is enough, you will maintain your peace, filled with hope and faith that greater days are ahead of you. It is that understanding that empowers you to stay peaceful. 1 Timothy 6:6 says, *"Now Godliness with contentment is great gain."* The recipe for being at peace in your life, regardless of your circumstance, is simply understanding you are going to make it through anything in the One (Jesus) who has given you everything.

I encourage you to start celebrating the goodness of God in your life. The Bible says, *"Rejoice in the Lord always. Again I will say, rejoice!"* God is good, not some of the time, but all of the time. And this good God is working on your behalf to give you a wonderful future. Instead of being worried, pray. Jesus said ask and you shall receive. He told us if we seek, we will find. The Bible says it is the effectual and fervent prayer of the righteous that avails much. This means prayer by Godly people gets results. Go to the Lord with your concerns, burdens and cares knowing He cares for you and provides for you. Anxiety will always abound when you think you are alone in overcoming life's challenges; but, you are not and you never will be. When you only rely on or trust in yourself, you will always feel burdened, stressed, overwhelmed or inadequate. These are recipes for emotional disaster. When you learn to trust God, you learn you are never alone, and you will never be dominated by a sense of inadequacy anymore. Walking with God means you walk in His wisdom, His power and His grace all the days of your life. It is amazing what happens when you allow Christ and His promises to displace inadequacy and worry as the focus of your attention. Fill your life with gratitude. Focus intently and passionately on who God is, what He promises you, and who He says you are. Meditate, day and night, on God's Word and not the world's. Meditate on what is good and not bad, what is lovely and not horrible, things to be grateful for and not things

241

to complain about. Before you know it, the peace of God which surpasses all understanding will be the rule of your life. It is simply a matter of trusting God's process. Listen to the amazing words of Jesus from the Sermon on the Mount in Matthew 5:5 (Message): *"You're blessed when you're content with just who you are—no more, no less. That's the moment you find yourselves proud owners of everything that can't be bought."* In the literal text of the Bible, the word "blessed" used here by Jesus means to be enviably happy and to be spiritually prosperous with life joy and satisfaction. God gave you peace so you can choose to be content everyday of your life. True joy and peace are found in Jesus, not possessions or circumstance, as evidenced by the Psalm below.

Psalms 4:1-8 (Message) — *"When I call, give me answers. God, take my side! Once, in a tight place, you gave me room; now I'm in trouble again: Grace me! Hear me! You rabble—how long do I put up with your scorn? How long will you lust after lies? How long will you live crazed by illusion? Look at this: look who got picked by God! He listens the split second I call to Him. Complain if you must, but don't lash out. Keep your mouth shut, and let your heart do the talking. Build your case before God and wait for His verdict. Why is everyone hungry for more? 'More, more,' they say. 'More, more.' I have God's more-than-enough, more joy in one ordinary day than they get in all their shopping sprees. At day's end I'm ready for sound sleep, for You, God, have put my life back together."*

Let me ask you a question: Is there an area of your life that you have wrongly become content with? Have you somehow convinced yourself to be at peace with not chasing your dreams? Have you settled for a so-so life? Have you, in any area of your life, accepted less than the fulfillment of God's promises for you? If there is ever anything to be discontent about, it is not living the abundant life of love, joy and peace that Jesus died on the cross for you to enjoy. Do not be discontent about possessions, be discontent that the enemy has robbed you of the life you desire. Do not settle for him winning. He is the loser in this battle. When the enemy attacks your life, fight back. Do not be content for letting him steal, kill or destroy your happiness. Do not be content with discontent. Do not accept anxiety, lack, worry or depression. Apply what you have now learned, trust the process God has laid out for you, and take a stand. It is time to get your hope back. It is time to get your excitement back. It is time to get your dreams back. It is time to get your future back.

Romans 5:17 (Message) — *"Can you imagine the breathtaking recovery life makes, sovereign life, in those who grasp with both hands this wildly extravagant life-gift, this grand setting-everything-right, that the one man Jesus Christ provides?"*

Life can get really complicated. Terrible things sometimes happen to really good people. Quite often, situations within or beyond our control come into our lives and it feels like we have lost so much. Sometimes people fall. Some people were raised by what can only be described as evil people, and their childhoods were filled with misery, abuse and torment. Occasionally, we make a series of unfortunate decisions that lead to the destruction of what we had planned for our futures. But, as you have just read, God is in the business of setting things right for you. Jesus does not come into your life to allow the wrongs to stay wrong. He takes what is wrong and makes it right. It is truly a wildly extravagant life-gift that His love for you has produced.

243

He says, "Can you imagine?" It is time to start imagining and believing for a new life filled with incredible possibilities, knowing God is going to do exceedingly and abundantly above anything you can ever ask, dream or desire. No more will you allow your imagination to be ruled by everything that has or could go wrong. **Recovery is available, and recovery is possible!** From this moment forward, your life is going to recover, but this is no ordinary recovery. God is going to give you a breathtaking recovery. You are going to be astonished by His goodness. You are going to be blown away by the mental and emotional healing He will provide. All you need to do is accept this gift. Please, do not reject it. Far too often, that is exactly the case. Too many people, including believers, do not or have not opened their hearts and minds to receive this gift of allowing Jesus to bring recovery into their lives by setting everything right. They live in pain. They live with a sense of devastation. They feel like life has been stolen from them and there is nothing to retrieve. It is completely understandable to see how you may have ended up feeling this way, but you no longer have to stay that way.

Is it possible to recover, to overcome, to heal and to get your life back? Yes, it is! God is with you and He is for you. Your future is not determined by your past. When you fall, you shall arise. You still have a great purpose and calling ahead of you. It is time to get back what the enemy tried to take away. You may have not reached your full potential to this point, but you can going forward. God declared over you a life of peace. He declared you can live with tranquility in your mind knowing you always have favor with Him. He promised to work on your behalf to deliver unto your life health, welfare, prosperity and all kinds of good things. He is the God of all blessing, and He has, is and always will pour out His blessing on your life.

The Bible says you are living in the most blessed time where God's free favors are abounding toward you in everything you do. If God promised this, you can believe for it and start moving toward it, but that means you must begin rejecting what has happened to you and start accepting what God is doing for you. It is far too easy to accept loss, pain, grief and disappointment as the rule of your life, but you do not need to anymore. Remember, guard your heart, for out of it flow the issues and boundaries of your life. How you respond to life is far more important than what happens to you in life. How are you going to respond now? Respond to this book in faith. Trust this process. In fact, let me say this: not only do you need to respond in faith, but you need to respond with action. Apply the process. Do not allow cynicism to talk you out of what God has proclaimed over you. Accept the amazing gift of allowing Him to bring recovery into your life today, but also move forward pursuing it. It is time to stop accepting the pain and loss, and start pursuing the life God has for you. It is time to recover. It is time to get your life back!

Acts 3:19–21 — *"Repent therefore and be converted, that your sins may be blotted out, so that times of refreshing may come from the presence of the Lord, and that He may send Jesus Christ, who was preached to you before, whom heaven must receive until the times of restoration of all things, which God has spoken by the mouth of all His holy prophets since the world began."*

I pray this book has initiated the times of refreshing God speaks of in these incredible scriptures. As you have read, the conclusion to the times of refreshing is the restoration of all things. God is the God of restoration. Everything that was lost, will be returned. Everything that was taken, will be brought back to you or replaced by something better. Do you believe it? I hope you do! God is going to restore your peace and your joy. Isaiah 54:10 says, *"For the mountains shall depart and the hills be removed, but My kindness shall not depart from you, nor shall My covenant of peace be removed."* There is nothing that can stop the peace of God gravitating toward you from Him. This is His promise. This is His covenant. You are not going to live broken. You are not going to live lost. You are not going to live hurting. You are not going to live decimated. You are not going to live disappointed. You are not going to live tormented and depressed anymore. Trust the process, accept the gift of recovery, and go live your best life. You can and you will get your life of peace back! No more missing peace.

245